ABSOLUTE ZERO GRAVITY:

SCIENCE JOKES, QUOTES, AND ANECDOTES

by Betsy Devine
and Joel E. Cohen

F

A FIRESIDE BOOK

Published by Simon & Schuster
New York London Toronto Sydney Tokyo Singapore

W9-AEZ-843

FIRESIDE
Simon & Schuster Building
Rockefeller Center
1230 Avenue of the Americas
New York, New York 10020

Designed by Quinn Hall
Manufactured in the United States of America

10 9 8 7 6 5 4 3 2 1

Library of Congress Cataloging-in-Publication Data

Devine, Betsy
    Absolute zero gravity / by Joel Cohen and Betsy Devine.
        p.   cm.
    "A Fireside book."
    1. Science—Humor.   I. Cohen, Joel E.   II. Title.
Q167.C65   1992
502'.07—dc20   92-21962
                                                        CIP

ISBN: 0-671-74060-1

The authors would like to make grateful acknowledgment for the use of the following published material:

Light Bulb Jokes (throughout) excerpted from the *Canonical Collection of Light Bulb Jokes*, copyright © 1988 Kurt Guntheroth. Used with permission of Kurt Guntheroth.

Lee DuBridge and Lord Kelvin quotes (p. 99), Sam Goldwyn quote (p. 144). From *A Stress Analysis of a Strapless Evening Gown*, Robert A. Baker (editor), Anchor Books, Doubleday and Co., 1963. Reprinted by permission of the publisher: Prentice-Hall/A Division of Simon & Schuster, Englewood Cliffs, New Jersey.

Darwin quotes (pp. 32, 67, 134). From *Charles Darwin and the Voyage of the Beagle*, Charles Robert Darwin, edited and with an introduction by Nora Barlow, Philosophical Library, 1946.

T. H. Huxley anecdotes (pp. 74, 75, 100). From *T. H. Huxley: Scientist, Humanist, & Educator*, by Cyril Bibby, C. W. Watts & Co., Ltd. 1959.

Linnaeus anecdotes (pp. 77–8). From *The Compleat Naturalist: A Life of Linnaeus*, Wilfred Blunt (with the assistance of William T. Stearn), Viking Press, 1971.

Mathematical greeting cards, bumper stickers, tombstones, light bulb joke table (pp. 37–8, 40, 42). Reprinted with permission from *SIAM News*: Volume 18, Number 5; Volume 19, Number 1; Volume 21, Number 6; Volume 22, Number 5; Volume 24, Number 3. "The Fifth Quadrant" competitions are edited by Richard Bronson and Gilbert Steiner.

permissions continued at back of book.

TABLE OF CONTENTS

Acknowledgments   6

Preface by Joel E. Cohen   7

Introductory Joke   9

Academia   10

The Scientific Personality   13

Scientific Specializations   22

Interdisciplinary Studies   47

Love, Sex, Marriage, and Scientists   56

Tales of the Great Scientists   64

Teaching Science   86

Scientific Reputations   99

Scientific Writing on the Walls   108

Medical Science   110

Publish or Perish   120

Scientific Product Warning Labels   123

Experimental Apparatus   125

The International Scientific Community   130

Women in Science   134

Food for Thought   137

Popular Science   141

Scientists in Heaven and Hell   145

Scientific Aphorisms   149

Logical Conclusions   151

Afterglow   155

Acknowledgments

Many thanks to:

Fred Almgren
Phil Anderson
William Anderson
Cathy Andrulis
Peter Astor
Krishna S. Athreya
John Biggs
Enrico Bombieri
Gaby Borel
Richard Bronson
Ray Brown
R. Eugene Burke
Hal Caswell
Dev Chen
David J. Cohen
Sidney Coleman
Paul Cranefield
David Damrosch
Bob Dempsey
Murray Devine
Kevin Devine
James Ebert
Paul Feit
Benji Fisher
Shelley Glashow
Paul Goldberg
Murph Goldberger
William T. Golden
Herman Goldstine
Anne Gonnella
Madelyn T. Gould
Claire Thomson Graaf
Raymond Greenwell
Victor Gribov
Kurt Guntheroth
Israel Halperin
Susan Hewitt
Charles Issawi
Nina Issawi
John Van Iwaarden
Jay Jorgenson
Steve Just
Mark Kac
Nick Khuri
Liz Khuri
Larry Knop
Joe Kohn
Manny Krasner
Peter Kronheimer
Sevda Kursunoglu
T. Kuster

Bob Langlands
Michael Larsen
Leon Lederman
Joe Lehner
David Leston
Gerri Lindner
Robert J. Lipshutz
Saunders MacLane
Gwendolyn Markus
Lawrence Markus
George Masnick
Frank McCullough
Sharon Johanson McCullough
E. J. McShane
Louise Morse
Dan Mostow
Chiara Nappi
Paul Nyiri
Ingram Olkin
Abraham Pais
Robert Parks
Jonathan Pila
Robert Pollak
Peter Ross
Mary Beth Ruskai
Amy Schoener
Daniel Seiver
Al Shapere
Ruby Sherr
Gus Simmons
Montgomery Slatkin
Gilbert Steiner
Edward Subitsky
Earl Taft
Alvin Thaler
Joan Treiman
Sam Treiman
Marvin Tretkoff
Albert W. Tucker
Paul Vojta
David Vondersmith
Edward Walters
André Weil
David Wendroff
Edward White
Ludmila Wightman
Mira Wilczek
Amity Wilczek
Frank Wilczek
Dick Wood
C. N. Yang
Peter Yodzis
Aki Yukie

PREFACE

When I was a freshman in college, I showed my calculus teacher a formula beloved by every high school scientist:

$$\int e^x = \mathfrak{f}(u^n).$$

(In case you can't read, this says: *sex = fun*. It's a freshman's idea of titillation.) He frowned. Then he said: "Doesn't the left side need a *dx*?" As I picked up my equation and left, I thought: "What a jerk! He thinks it's mathematics!" Thirty years later, I wondered whether I had been had. Maybe my section man saw that the equation said *sex = fun*. Maybe he was pretending to take it seriously. If so, I swallowed his act.

Scientists are funny people. Not just the great ones who think they've discovered the secret of life or of the brain or of the common cold. Even ordinary day-to-day scientists are funny, because they all think that *the world makes sense*! Most people know better.

In pursuit of their delusion, scientists have developed some pretty strange habits of thought and behavior. They constantly act as if *things have explanations*. This article of faith is very weakly supported by day-to-day experience. To justify this credo, scientists ignore all the things that don't have explanations (take your choice). They expend no end of the taxpayer's money to isolate, build walls around, and study intensely the few crumbs of life that do have explanations.

Scientists also insist that other people have to be able to understand their explanations. *Scientists are forever explaining things to each other*. They publish thousands of scientific journals with hundreds of thousands of articles, each read by two of the authors' friends and three of their enemies and an occasional, mad graduate student. They swarm, like bees in search of a nesting site, from one scientific meeting to another, shifting restlessly from one lecture to another, from a transparency with numbers too small to read to equations with notation too complex to comprehend—explaining and trying to grasp explanations. Scientists are just as good at explaining things convincingly as the director of the CIA, the chairman of the KGB, the president of any tobacco company, certain religious leaders, and other revered figures of public and private life.

The reason that scientific explanations sound so strange is that they are. Let me explain. Daily life is a jumble. (You noticed that, too?) Therefore the parts of experience that make sense and have explanations don't have a lot to do with daily life. So *scientists invent new language*—new words, new conventions about words, plus new symbols and conventions about symbols—to describe the rare parts of life that make sense. (To be a properly formed mathematical expression, $\int e^x$ needs a dx, my calculus teacher told me, as if I didn't know.) When it comes to explaining these esoteric descriptions, strange concepts are invented, exploited, enshrined, and discarded. Most of these concepts would never be entertained seriously by any practical person with her or his feet on the ground. (Phlogiston, the ether, and phrenology are merely the whipping boys of retrospective wisdom. It's a safe bet that 80 percent of today's explanatory concepts—mind you, not the ones I've proposed, but maybe some of yours, and certainly most of his—will seem absurd in fifty years, if anyone then can even remember them.) Like firework rockets launched at night, scientific concepts streak out of nowhere, glitter, and are gone. They are useful for all that, because they lift scientists' attention skyward and feed their hopes.

Because this is a book of humor and anecdotes about science and scientists (in addition to a considerable number of jokes we just happened to like), there are lots of stories about the work of making sense of the world, about explanations and the people who give them (sometimes known as teachers), and about the wild language and weird concepts of scientific explanations.

But one thing we do not dare to tell jokes about: *science is serious.* No joke. If my colleagues ever see this book, do you know what they'll say? "It's his greatest contribution to science," and the career of one working scientist goes in the trash. (It's okay for Betsy to write a scientific joke book; after all, she's a writer and a historian.) No, sir! You cannot take time out from making measurements and calculations and theorems and hypotheses to tell jokes about the seriousness of science. If you tell jokes, maybe all those people who aren't so sure that the world makes sense might be on to something.

So please, folks, buy this book, read it, and enjoy it. But don't show it to my colleagues.

Joel E. Cohen

INTRODUCTORY JOKE

A young scientist whose boyfriend was an aspiring comedian went with him to the jokewriters' annual convention, expecting to hear some fantastic stories. Instead, the featured comic began to rattle off a series of numbers.

"Ninety-three!" said the speaker, and the audience chuckled appreciatively. "Two hundred twelve!" They laughed again. "One thousand thirty-seven!" More laughter.

The scientist couldn't stand it any longer. She nudged her friend and whispered, "What's going on?"

"Simple," he said. "You see, every joke in the world has been catalogued and given a number. When one of us says 'Ninety-three,' that means *joke* number ninety-three. So we laugh. Get it?"

"You mean," asked the scientist dubiously, "you're going to crack up if I say to you, 'Twenty-six'?"

"No, no," said the boyfriend, "your delivery is wrong. Listen to this guy. He's good and you might learn something."

So the scientist tried to appreciate the comedian's technique on forty-six, nine hundred eighty-nine, and two thousand five hundred thirty-six. Then the comedian paused dramatically, waving his hands for silence. When he had the audience's full attention, he shouted "Ten thousand—two hundred—and three!" There was pandemonium. People clapped and cheered. The scientist's boyfriend was laughing so hard that tears ran down his face and he could hardly stand.

"What happened? What happened?" she demanded. "Why was that one so funny?"

"Well," said her friend, "we never *heard* that joke before!"

ACADEMIA

TO BE FAIR, WE ADMIT THAT MOST OF THEM CAN SPELL THEIR JOB TITLES

In any academic setting, the scientists get along like a great big happy family—with lots of bickering. Engineers tell physicist jokes, physicists tell mathematician jokes, mathematicians tell engineer jokes, and it all goes around and around. But one thing all the scientists agree on is telling dean jokes. Like, did you hear about the dean who was so confused that the *other* deans noticed?

Or how about this one: Santa Claus, the Easter Bunny, an intelligent dean, and a stupid dean were locked in an office with no key. Which one discovered a clever way for them all to get out?

Believe it or not, it was the stupid dean—because Santa Claus, the Easter Bunny, and an intelligent dean do not exist.

THE DEAN OF ACADEMIC LIGHT BULB JOKES

How many deans does it take to change a light bulb?

Two. One to assure the faculty that everything possible is being done, while the other screws the bulb into a faucet.

JUST A FEW MORE ITERATIONS AND SOMEBODY WILL HIRE A DEAN

André Weil's Law of Faculties: First-rate people hire other first-rate people. Second-rate people hire third-rate people. Third-rate people hire fifth-rate people.

AND IF YOU'RE WONDERING WHAT THE ADMINISTRATION THINKS
OF THE FACULTY . . .

A professor from France had just arrived in Princeton, and was being escorted along University Place. "Those Gothic palaces, who lives in them?" he asked, pointing to one of the university's more grandly gargoyled dormitories.

"Housing for students," replied his friend.

On the other side of the road, some townhouses for junior faculty caught his eye. "And these simple dwellings, who lives there?" he asked.

"Faculty members," replied his friend.

The Frenchman rolled his eyes from one to the other and shook his head as if to clear it. "Quelle chose curieuse," said he.

THE CREATION

In the Beginning was the Plan;
And then came the Assumptions;
And the Assumptions were without Form;
And the Plan was completely without Substance;
And Darkness came upon the faces of the Faculty,
And so they spoke unto their Department Heads, saying,
"It is a Crock of S—t, and it Stinketh!"
And the Department Heads sought out their Deans,
And spoke softly, saying,
"It is a Container of Excrement, and Verily, it is most Strong,
Such that none here may abide it."
And the Deans went before the Provost, bowing low, and crying,
"It is a Vessel of Fertilizer, such that None may abide its Strength."
And the Provost stood before the President,
On bended Knee, wailing,
"It contains that which aideth the Growth of Plants,
and it is very Strong."
And the President went in unto the Trustees and humbly said,
"This powerful Plan will augment our Building Fund,
That all may Glorify the Wisdom of this Board."
And the Trustees looked upon the Plan and saw that it was Good,
And in this manner did the Plan become Policy.

At one university, they never schedule a faculty meeting on a Wednesday because it kills two weekends.

At another, they never schedule a faculty meeting for December because it kills two summers.

---

and the answer is:
July and August

and the question is:
Name two great reasons to become an academic.

THE SCIENTIFIC PERSONALITY

Youthful Enthusiam

DOING WHAT COMES NATURALIST-ICALLY

Louis Agassiz was a gifted and inspiring teacher. Edward Lurie records the impression of a hack driver who drove one of Agassiz's Harvard classes on a naturalizing excursion: "I drove the queerest lot you ever saw. They chattered like monkeys. They jumped the fences, tore about the fields, and came back with their hats covered with bugs. I asked their keeper what ailed them; he said they were naturals, and judgin' from the way they acted I should say they were."

ON THE ORDER OF SIXTEEN WAYS TO SPOT A SCIENCE NERD*

1. They stand in the rain watching it drip in front of lights and say, "Oh, wow, look at the acceleration."
2. They get scared walking into the theater department library.
3. They say, "Oh, good, we don't have any plans for Friday—we can work on astronomy all day."
4. They have pizza delivered to the science building.
5. Their idea of rebellion is to go to the blackboard and draw astronomical symbols upside down.
6. They refer to printed documents (i.e., papers) as "hardcopies."
7. As they sleep, they find themselves typing out their dream dialogues.

* A longer version of this list originally appeared on the teleJoke conference on the GEnie network.

8. They sit centimeters (not inches) apart at a desk with two computers and send each other messages by electronic mail instead of by talking.
9. They refer to their friends by their e-mail addresses.
10. They explain to their four-year-old cousins the difference between velocity and speed.
11. They see a Slinky and think of simple harmonic motion.
12. They use insults like: "You are three sigma from the mean, you symbolic stack dump!"
13. They say, "I'll be there at 3 P.M. plus or minus 15 minutes."
14. They realize that if you drive fast enough toward a red light it will actually be green.
15. They think of writing letters by hand as "the analog method."
16. They sit at the console and type dumb lists about nerds just so their fingers can be happy typing.

and the answer is:
Annoyed.

and the question is:
What do you call a science nerd from Brooklyn
(especially after he hears this joke)?

MAXWELL RUNS THE GAUNTLET

James Clerk Maxwell (1831–1879) was the author of the famous equations describing the interaction of electric and magnetic forces, which might today be known as "Clerk's Equations" if his father had not followed the ancient Scottish custom of adding a new surname when he acquired a legacy.

As a child, Maxwell pestered his mother constantly with the question, "What's the go of that?" If her answer was not satisfactory, he persisted, "But what is the *particular* go of that?" His curiosity and eccentric sense of humor earned him the schoolboy nickname of "Daftie."

Maxwell was only fourteen years old when his first paper was read to the Royal Society of Edinburgh. As a student at Cambridge University, young Maxwell performed some unusual experiments on his own internal clock. He would work far into the small hours, then refresh himself with an hour of physical exercise, racing a circuit of dormitory halls and stairways. His fellow-students finally dissuaded him by pelting him with boots and brushes as he passed.

Eccentricities

THANKS, BUT I MIGHT BE ABLE TO FIND A DRUNK CABDRIVER WHO SPEAKS NO ENGLISH

Norbert Wiener was both absent-minded and near-sighted, a combination that made him a menace behind the wheel of a car. The story is told that once a French mathematician visiting M. I. T. was invited to a nearby party. He accepted Wiener's offer of a ride, and disaster swiftly followed. After several terrifying near-misses, Wiener demolished the car against a telephone pole. While Wiener talked to police, the Frenchman, miraculously uninjured, walked the rest of the way to his party.

A couple of hours later the Frenchman was quite enjoying himself. Then, from nowhere, Wiener appeared at his side. "Don't worry," Wiener told him, smiling mistily over his glass. "I've managed to borrow another car. Whenever you want to go, I can drive you back!"

POSSIBLE HAZARDS OF SCIENTIFIC TRAINING

In Europe, one can go from one's home to an international conference with merely a long train ride in between. One scientist, after such a trip, came home looking ashen and distraught.

"What happened?" asked his wife.

"My dear," groaned the scientist, "I have been riding for hours in a backward-facing seat—you know how that always distresses my liver."

"But, darling," said his wife, "we have talked of this before, and surely you told me that if you found yourself in such a spot, you would ask the person in the seat facing you to exchange places."

"Alas," said the scientist. "On this trip I could not ask. There was no one sitting there."

DOWNS AND UPS OF MY NAVAL CAREER

Sounds unlikely to me, but according to this story a mathematician became captain of the kind of ship that actually sinks on purpose—a submarine. His briefing speech to new sailors went as follows: "I have developed a simple method that you would do well to learn. Every day, count the number of times the submarine has dived since you boarded. Add to this the number of times it has surfaced. If the sum you arrive at is not an even number—don't open the hatches!"

NO, I THINK YOU WERE SITTING A PARSEC AWAY

A young astrophysicist out on a very rare date excused himself and wandered off to the men's room. A few minutes later he returned, peering about near-sightedly. "Excuse me," he said to a pretty blonde drinking a glass of wine. "Did I knock over your glass earlier this evening?"

"You certainly did," she replied.

"Good," he said, plunking himself down across from her. "This is my table."

PARLOR GAME THEORY

The great era of parties in Princeton has gone by. The topologist J. W. Alexander is said to have given a winter beach party where truckloads of sand were dumped on his living room rug for the guests to carouse on—wearing their bathing suits, as my informant told me, during the *early* part of the evening.

John von Neumann also gave famous cocktail parties that sometimes resulted in young mathematicians who were unable to find their way home again being put to bed upstairs. A young mathematician strolled up to von Neumann at one of these parties and asked, "Say, is there somewhere around here I can go to the toilet?"

"As a matter of fact," said von Neumann graciously, "we have a room especially for that purpose."

IGOR IS THE STUPID ONE, I'M SUPPOSED TO BE THE SMART ONE

A certain scientist had progressed all the way to being a mad scientist and was finally committed to an institution. One day while out for a stroll, he saw through the fence a motorist changing a tire. The motorist, unnerved to discover a patient so near at hand, stepped on the hubcap containing his tire's lugnuts, and watched in dismay as all four clattered down a storm sewer.

The scientist cleared his throat. "If you take just one lugnut off each of the other three tires," he said, "it will give you three extras to put on your spare. Then you could drive to a gas station and get some more."

The motorist was amazed. "That's a wonderful idea! How did you ever think of that?"

"I'm here because I'm crazy," said the scientist drily, "not because I'm stupid."

THE HONOR WAS NOT FOR HIS KNOWLEDGE OF CURRENT EVENTS
The French physicist Ampère (1775–1836), whose name is now used for the unit of electric current, was remarkable for his absent-mindedness. He did not even recognize Napoleon, who came one day to visit the Paris Academy and the great Ampère. Smiling, Napoleon commanded Ampère to join him for dinner at the Palace the next day—that should make his face more familiar! Perhaps it would have if Ampère had gone. But he had already forgotten the invitation.

PRONOUNCING IT "SHLEEPING" DOESN'T MAKE IT BETTER
When he was a little boy growing up in Budapest, the mathematician Paul Erdös set out to teach himself English. Unfortunately, his book did not explain that the rules of pronunciation are quite different in English and in Hungarian. For example, in Hungarian the letter c is pronounced ts, s is pronounced sh, and there is no silent e. So the language that Erdös in fact taught himself was "Erdös English"—English words pronounced as if they were Hungarian.

In Erdös English, ice cubes become *its-eh tsu-besh*, and used cars are *u-shed tsarsh*.

Perhaps the most famous of many eccentric-Erdös stories is the following: Erdös had intended to be away overnight, but later decided to take the late train back that evening after all. So when he caught sight of his landlady near the train station, it seemed a good time to tell her about his change of plans. "Oh, Mrs. Green," he shouted across the street, "it turns out that tonight again I will be sleeping with you!"

Sleeping Habits

I THINK, THEREFORE I THINK I'LL STAY IN BED
Scientists who hate to get up early can point to the sad fate of René Descartes (1596–1650), the father of analytic geometry. Descartes showed genius even as a schoolboy, when he succeeded in convincing his Jesuit schoolmasters that he should never be asked to get out of bed before 11. This custom he followed throughout a long and busy military career, his superior officers being no more able than his teachers to interfere with his peaceful morning habits. Descartes

later claimed that all his great scientific and philosophical works were composed during the mornings he spent in bed. (So, no doubt, was his treatise on the art of dueling, the only one of all his books that the Catholic Church did *not* proscribe after his death.)

This happy life was changed in 1649, when Queen Christina of Sweden invited him to Stockholm to instruct her in geometry. Unfortunately, her royal schedule demanded that these teaching sessions take place at 5 A.M. The shock of getting up so early and walking through the frigid winter darkness to her palace gave him pneumonia, and he died on February 11, 1650.

IF DESCARTES HAD BEEN LISTENING, HE WOULD HAVE CALLED IN TO EXPRESS HIS SUPPORT

Very early on the morning of October 15, 1979, physicist Sheldon Glashow's telephone rang. "Good morning!" said a cheery Boston voice. "I wonder if you would like to tell our radio listeners how you feel about winning the Nobel Prize in physics?"

"I feel sleepy," mumbled Glashow, and hung up.

AND IF HE DID, HE'D BE IN NO SHAPE TO TEACH ANYWAY

Wolfgang Pauli's department chairman once asked him to teach a 9 A.M. class. "Impossible," snapped Pauli. "I never stay up so late."

The Scientist as Social Animal

A UNIT SO SMALL ONE WONDERED HOW DIRAC COULD FUNCTION

The dons at St. John's of Cambridge, when P. A. M. Dirac was a fellow there, decided to coin a new unit: the dirac. One dirac represents the smallest measurable amount of conversation—so a silent colleague might be described as "only a 20-dirac chap."

In Göttingen, the same idea was expressed somewhat differently: "There is no god, and Dirac is his prophet."

MATHEMATICS IS NOT A SOCIAL SCIENCE

Paul Erdös tells the story that in 1937 he and Paul Turán went to visit a mathematician friend who was suffering from paranoia. They knocked on his door. After a long while it opened just a crack, and the friend's voice whispered, "Please come again, but at another time, and to another person."

BESIDES, MAILMEN ANNOY GREAT DANES

Niels Bohr hated having to write letters and always put it off as long as possible. One day his brother Harald noticed on his desk a letter that should have been sent long ago. Urged to put it in an envelope and mail it, Niels protested, "Oh no, that is just one of the first drafts for a rough copy!"

IT WASN'T SO MUCH HIS QUESTION AS HOW HE ASKED IT

Wolfgang Pauli and Eugene Wigner are two Nobel Prize–winning physicists, one famous for his rudeness and the other for his politeness. So you are entitled to wonder if this story is apocryphal. We heard it was true.

Pauli gave a seminar and afterwards asked for questions. Wigner stood up and hesitantly began, "Excuse me, but I was just wondering if perhaps you—"

"No, no, no!" thundered Pauli, cutting him off. "Certainly not, you're absolutely wrong." A pause. "What is the question?"

THE VERY QUESTION SO MANY WERE DYING TO ASK PAULI

More on Wigner's politeness. It is said that once in his life even Wigner reached the end of his tether, when he went to pick up his car from the repair shop and discovered the bill was nearly twice what he had been quoted. Very hesitantly, he asked the mechanic if there might not be some mistake. The mechanic replied with a long and loud harangue about the miserliness of idiot professors, especially foreign ones. So Wigner paid the full amount and turned to go. Then he turned back and said, "But—excuse me—might I just ask you to go to hell, please?"

IN WHICH CASE, HOW DARE YOU ASK HIM *ANY* QUESTIONS?

Not many theoretical physicists can do experiments, and some people claim there is a negative correlation—the greater the theorist, the worse he is in a laboratory. But everyone admits Pauli was unusually heavy-handed. To let him touch your apparatus spelled certain doom, and even to have him walk into your lab put the experiment at risk.

One day, in James Franck's laboratory at Göttingen, his experimental set-up just exploded for no apparent reason. Later Franck learned that Pauli had been en route from Zurich to Copenhagen that day. The disaster had occurred as his train paused for five minutes at the Göttingen train station. The sheer magnitude of this effect caused many to say Pauli must be the greatest theoretical physicist of all time.

Arrogance

NO PROFESSION OF IGNORANCE

Back in the days when Los Alamos was a small company town, a noted theoretical physicist was called as a witness for the prosecution. Rising to take the stand, the great man smiled and nodded affably in the direction of the jury box. This infuriated counsel for the defense. "Your Honor, I don't see how my client can get a fair trial here," he said angrily. Turning to the professor, he demanded, "I want your answer, and remember that you are under oath. Do you, or do you not, know more than half the members of this jury?"

The physicist smiled. "Under oath, I can easily swear I know more than all of them put together."

OR WOULD YOU RATHER I GAVE YOU AN EXAMPLE?

A theoretical physicist had been told that only a miracle could cure his arrogance, so he decided to try for one: "Dear God, please make me less arrogant. By the way, God, let me remind you that the word 'arrogant' should be defined as follows . . ."

AND THEN RUN VERY FAST?

THEORETICAL PHYSICIST: Did you hear the latest joke about the experimental physicist?

STRANGER: Perhaps I should warn you that I am an experimental physicist.

THEORETICAL PHYSICIST: Thanks for the warning, I'll tell it very slowly.

THE PEAK OF ARROGANCE

An experimental physicist and a theoretical physicist went hiking together. Needless to say, they were soon lost in the mountains. After several hours of aimless wandering, the theorist commandeered the map and studied it for about fifteen minutes. "Boy, are you stupid," he told his friend. He pointed across the valley. "You see that big mountain peak over there? *That's* where we are!"

VIVE LA DIFFÉRENCE!

The mechanical "difference engine" of Charles Babbage (1792–1871) was an early precursor of the computer. An educated and fascinating man, Babbage became a favorite in London literary circles. Among his close friends was the great Victorian poet laureate, Alfred Lord Tennyson, and there survives an extraordinary letter from Babbage to Tennyson, provoked by a poetry reading.

"Every moment dies a man, Every moment one is born," proclaimed Tennyson in his poem "The Vision of Sin." Babbage, dismayed by this careless mathematical misstatement, begged him to replace the offending lines with "Every moment there dies a man, And one and a sixth is born."

Babbage modestly admitted that his own lines also contained a small inaccuracy—"the exact figures are 1.167, but something must, of course, be conceded to the laws of metre."

SCIENTIFIC SPECIALIZATIONS

Anatomy

MIDNIGHT BEDEVILMENT

During the bloody years after the French Revolution, the great comparative anatomist Georges Cuvier (1769–1832) took refuge in a tutoring job. One young student, deciding to play a trick on him, disguised himself as a devil and crept into the master's bedroom at midnight. "Ahhhh! Cuvier!" he wailed. "Cuvier, I am going to eat you!"

Cuvier opened sleepy eyes and protested, "Horns? Hooves? *Herbivore*—you can't!"

Astronomy

UP, UP AND AWAY

Did you hear the one about the NASA rocket that lost its job? Some scientists decided to get it fired.

SOMEBODY FIRE THAT PHILOSOPHER!

The 1801 discovery of Ceres, largest of many minor planets in the asteroid belt, came as no surprise to astronomers, who had predicted a "missing" planet in the gap between Mars and Jupiter. Another event of the intellectual year: Hegel published a philosophical proof that the solar system could contain no more than the seven planets known from antiquity.

SOMETHING HEGEL CLEARLY DIDN'T KNOW

This mnemonic helps students remember the names of the solar system's nine major planets: My Very Educated Mother Just Served Us Nine Pizzas. (Mercury, Venus, Earth, Mars, Jupiter, Saturn, Uranus, Neptune, and Pluto, in case it *didn't* help you remember.)

HECK, SHE'LL HAVE TO USE HER HEADLIGHTS

The NASA scientist's preschooler told him proudly that she intended to be an astronaut. But none of this messing around on the moon for her. She'd be the first woman to land on the sun.

"But, honey," he said, "you can't land on the sun. It's too hot, it would melt your rocket."

She thought about this for a minute. "Good point," she agreed. "I'd better go at night."

TO BOLDLY GO WHERE NO LIGHT BULB JOKE HAS GONE BEFORE

How many members of the USS Enterprise does it take to change a light bulb?

Scotty will report to Captain Kirk
that the light bulb in the Engineering Section is burnt out.
Scotty, after checking around, notices that they have no new light
bulbs, and complains that he can't see in the dark to tend
to his engines.
Kirk must order an emergency stop
at the next uncharted planet, Alpha Regula IV,
to procure a light bulb from the natives.
Kirk, Spock, Bones, Sulu, and three security officers beam down.
The three security officers are promptly killed by the natives,
and the rest of the landing party is captured.
(Meanwhile, back on the Enterprise, Scotty has sighted a Klingon
ship and has had to warp out of orbit to escape detection.)
Bones cures the native king, who is suffering from the flu,
and as a reward the landing party is set free and given all the light
bulbs they can carry.
Scotty cripples the Klingon ship and warps back to the planet
just in time to beam up Kirk and his landing party.
The new bulb is inserted,
and the Enterprise proudly continues on its mission.

How many Vulcans does it take to change a light bulb?
Approximately 1.000000

> How many astronomers does it take to change a light bulb?
> *Change a light bulb? What's wrong with the dark?*

Biology

A WOMAN WITHOUT A MAN IS LIKE A MARTIAN WITHOUT
A BICYCLE?

A team of Earth biologists is sent to Mars, where a team of Martian biologists is waiting to meet them. The two groups discuss at great length all aspects of life on their different planets. Finally, after full rapport has been carefully established, the Earth team asks about sex.

The number of ceremonies and procedures it takes for the three Martian sexes to get together takes half an hour to describe, but the earthlings listen with great respect, taking notes on every complicated detail.

Then the Martians want to know about sex on Earth. The Earth biologists begin to explain, but to their chagrin the Martians soon start giggling, then laughing, then rolling around on the floor in helpless glee.

"Sorry—sorry!" gasps the chief Martian scientist. "It's just that— what you're describing is how we make bicycles!"

POLAR OPPOSITES

Then there was the Antarctic biologist who went to spend a year in Alaska. Trouble is, he drove his colleagues crazy with stories about how soft they had it compared with the *real* men he was used to working with. One night when a howling wind blew gusts of snow through every crack in their Quonset hut, the visitor went too far. "Hardly worth building up the fire on a mild spring night like this," he remarked. "Down around Ross Island, *real* men . . ."

"Listen, pal," grunted a heavily-bearded caribou specialist, "why don't you lay off that stuff? Up here *our* idea of a real man is someone who can drink a full bottle of whiskey, make love to a woman all night, and wrestle a polar bear with his bare hands."

"Oh, is that all it takes?" said the South Poler scornfully. He strode over to the stores cupboard, pulled out a fifth of whiskey and drained it to the bottom. "Polar bear cave about a mile north of here as I recall?" he asked nonchalantly, and strolled off into the storm.

Time passed, a lot of time passed, enough time passed for people to have stopped taking bets on how fast he'd come back and started talking about a search party. The South Pole man staggered in through the door, and he was a terrible sight. One boot and both mittens were gone, his parka spouted goose down where giant claws had ripped it, one eye was closed and swelling fast. Unbelievably, the man still smiled.

"So much for the polar bear," he said. "Now, where's this woman I've got to wrestle?"

The original scientific "guinea pig" was used by Pierre Simon Laplace (1749–1827), better known for his work in mathematical physics, to show that in respiration as in combustion, oxygen combines with food (or fuel) to give off heat.

Dyslexic insomniac agnostic: someone who stays up all night to ponder the meaning of D-O-G.

---

and the question is:
Why does an anteater never get sick?

and the answer is:
Because its stomach is full of antibodies.

ECONOMY OF NATURE
Know, Nature's children shall divide her care:
The fur that warms a monarch warmed a bear.
While Man exclaims, "See all things for my use!"
"See man for mine," replies a pamper'd goose.
                                    ALEXANDER POPE

Chemistry

WE KNEW THERE WAS SOMETHING WRONG WITH KP CHEMISTRY!
The sergeant is training his hapless assistants in practical science. "Now this is important: water boils at ninety degrees."

One private raises a timid hand. "Please, sir, please! I am an assistant professor of chemistry and I must tell you that water boils at one hundred degrees."

"Ahem!" the sergeant clears his throat. "One hundred degrees, of course. Ninety degrees is where the right angle boils."

THE LOGIC OF CHEMISTRY

CHEMISTRY PROFESSOR: Now, class, here I have a beaker of H_2SO_4, and here I have a gold ring. Suppose I drop the ring into the sulfuric acid. Will the gold dissolve?

STUDENT: No.

PROFESSOR: Good. And will you please tell us why not?

STUDENT: If it would dissolve, you wouldn't put it in.

---

and the question is:
Name these molecules.

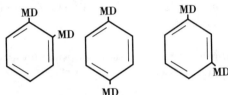

and the answer is:
Orthodox, paradox . . . and metaphysicians.

WOULD YOU BELIEVE, A FERROUS WHEEL?

Computer Science

SCIENTISTS-MEET-SHAGGY-DOG STORY

Back in the 1940s, when having a computer meant putting together your own room-sized assemblage of wires and tubes, John von Neumann decided that the Institute for Advanced Study would be the ideal place for one. Through the grapevine, he learned that the best man in the country to help him build one was a world-class tinkerer named Julian Bigelow. So von Neumann invited Bigelow to visit.

At last the day came when Bigelow knocked on the door. As von Neumann opened it, in romped a big, friendly dog of indeterminate breed. The men talked for an hour, with the dog barking around their feet. Then Bigelow got up to leave, shook hands, and headed for his car. "Wait a minute," said von Neumann, "aren't you going to take your dog?"

"My dog?" said Bigelow. "I thought he was your dog."

FIRST LAW OF COMPUTER SANITY
(FORMULATED BY VON NEUMANN)
In a day consisting of twenty-four hours, it is desirable that any computer should require less than twenty-four hours of maintenance.

---

and the question is:
What couple had the first his-and-hers computers?

and the answer is:
Adam and Eve. She had an Apple and he had a Wang.

COMPUTER START-UP COMPANIES FROM HELL
Did you hear about the computer start-up in Idaho that went nowhere even faster than most? Seems they based their hardware on a potato chip.

How's this for a super-computer promise: Our machine is so fast it can process an infinite loop in 4.8 seconds.

How about the start-up group from Texas? Their selling point: in the whole world you won't find a bigger microcomputer!

LIGHT BULB JOKES TO TURN ON YOUR FAVORITE MAINFRAME
How many programmers does it take to change a light bulb?
None, that's a hardware problem.
(Alternative answer)
Two, because one is sure to leave in the middle of the project.
How many data-base people does it take to change a light bulb?
Three. One to write the light bulb removal program,
one to write the light bulb insertion program,
and one to act as a light bulb administrator to make
sure nobody else
tries to change the light bulb at the same time.
How many technical writers does it take to change a light bulb?
Only one, but there has to be a programmer around
to explain how to do it.
How many UNIX hacks does it take to change a light bulb?
As many as you want, they're all virtual anyway.

How many Bell Labs vice presidents does it take to change
a light bulb?
Sorry, but that's proprietary information.

How many IBM employees does it take to change a light bulb?
*One hundred. Ten to do it, and ninety to write Document Number
GC7500439-0001, Multitasking Incandescent System Facility,
of which 10 percent of the pages state only
"This page intentionally left blank,"
and 20 percent of the definitions are of the form
"A . . . consists of sequences of nonblank characters
separated by blanks."*

How many computer network users does it take to submit a new
light bulb joke?
*One thousand. One to come up with a new one,
while 999 submit,
"How many programmers does it take to change a light bulb? None,
that's a hardware problem."*

DAVE? I'M SCARED, DAVE

The cyberneticist sat back in his airplane seat and beamed. Take-off had gone without a hitch. Then over the loudspeaker came a melodious electronic voice that he had programmed: "Ladies and gentlemen, you have the honor to be present at the world's first fully automated airplane flight. Every member of the flight crew today, from the pilot down to the stewards, is a specially programmed electronic robot. Once again, technology has stepped in to remove the possibility of any human error. So sit back, relax, and enjoy this evening's movie. Nothing at all can go wrong, go wrong, go wrong, go wrong . . ."

COMPUTER EXPERT–TEASING

What's the difference between a computer expert and a novice? The novice hesitates a minute before doing something stupid.

What's the difference between a computer expert and a used-car salesman? When a used-car salesman is lying to you, he knows it.

How can you spot a real computer expert? A real computer expert can make a mistake and not get mad at the computer.

BYTE THE HAND THAT FEEDS YOU?
The hardware engineer's favorite kind of cookie? Chocolate chip of course!

NEITHER KIND IS WILLING TO DISK-CUSS IT
There are only two kinds of computer users: those who have lost important data in a hardware crash and those who are about to.

MAYBE HE SAW "HARDBODIES" ONCE TOO OFTEN
Then there was the football player who got kicked out of his cybernetics lab the third time they caught him trying to make a robot.

ARTIFICIAL INTELLIGENCE: A SAD-BUT-TRUISM
Artificial intelligence will never be a match for natural stupidity.

---

and the question is:
Why are computer viruses so dangerous?

and the answer is:
They could give you a terminal illness.

Demography

SO LET'S MAKE THE WORLD SAFE FOR DEMOGRAPHY
A demographer is someone who explains how you can have a thousand people at a cocktail party in a telephone booth if nobody stays too long.

IS THAT A COMPUTER IN YOUR PHONE BOOTH OR ARE YOU GLAD TO SEE ME?
What is the difference between a demographer
and a mathematical demographer?
*A demographer makes wild guesses about the future of populations.
A mathematical demographer uses computers and statistics
to make wild guesses about the future of populations.*

and the answer is:
Count Dracula

and the question is:
What did Transylvania's only demographer forget to do?

Economics

JOEL'S LAWS OF ECONOMICS
First law: For every economist, there is an equal and opposite
economist.
Second law: They are both wrong.

and the answer is:
Trouble

and the question is:
Name the one commodity where supply always exceeds the
demand.

ECONOMICS OF LIGHT BULB JOKES

How many economists does it take to change a light bulb?
*Two. One to assume the ladder and the other to
change the bulb.*

How many supply-side economists does it take to screw in
a light bulb?
*None. And if the government would just leave it alone, it would
screw itself in.*

How many accountants does it take to change a light bulb?
What kind of answer do you need?

How many Marxist economists does it take to screw in
a light bulb?
None. The bulb contains the seeds of its own revolution.

Economist: someone who knows more about money than the people
who have it.

Engineering

WHO ENGINEERED THESE LIGHT BULB JOKES?

How many nuclear engineers does it take to
change a light bulb?

*Seven. One to install the bulb and six to figure out
what to do with the old bulb for the next ten thousand years.*

How many field service engineers does it take to change
a light bulb?

It depends on how many defective bulbs they brought.

How many managing engineers does it take to change a light bulb?

*Three. One to procure the bulb by calling supply, one to call a
subordinate to install it, and one to look up the relevant
phone numbers.*

How many ergonomicists does it take to change a light bulb?

Five, four of them to decide which way the bulb ought to turn.

How many consulting engineers does it take to change
a light bulb?

One. That will be fifty dollars, please.

How many efficiency experts does it take to change a light bulb?

None. Efficiency experts change only dark *bulbs.*

Entomology

HE LOVES 'EM, YEAH, YEAH, YEAH

Human curiosity is a funny thing. How else to explain the fact that reporters always want to know what clergymen think about sex, and what biologists think about God?

The distinguished British geneticist J. B. S. Haldane (1892–1964) was asked a somewhat fancier version of the usual question. "You have spent a lifetime gazing into the face of Nature," legend quotes his interviewer. "Can you tell us what you have learned about the mind of God?"

Haldane puzzled over this for a minute. "I'm really not sure," he said, "except that He must have an inordinate fondness for beetles."

I ALWAYS THOUGHT THERE WAS SOMETHING GODLIKE ABOUT DARWIN

During Darwin's years at Cambridge, he spent many hours beetle-collecting in the Cambridge fens. One day, under the bark of an old tree trunk he discovered not one but two rare beetles. He had just caught one of them in each hand when a third appeared. Quickly, Darwin freed his right hand by popping that beetle into his mouth.

Sad to say, it was just as quick to react, by squirting out some slimy, bitter juice. Darwin lost it and the third one got away as well.

---

and the question is:
Why did the beetle jump over the cliff?

and the answer is:
It was trying to commit insecticide.

Genetics

GENETIC INVARIANCE

A genetics professor at the University of Wisconsin tells the following story: After his introductory lecture, an older student came up with a question. She had taken the same course from him years before—should she sit in on it again before taking exams for med school?

"That depends on how much you remember from before," he said. "Genetics hasn't really changed that much."

"On the contrary!" she replied. "From your lecture today, I see everything has changed—except your jokes."

A QUESTION OF CHROMOSOMES, DON'T ASK HIM Y

A prince out for a ride in his carriage caught sight of a man who looked very much like him. He called the man over and asked him curiously, "Tell me, was your mother ever in service at the palace?"

Holding himself very straight, the commoner replied, "No, your majesty. But my father was."

Geology

ALL FIELD TRIPS HAVE THEIR UPS AND DOWNS

The geology class was let loose on a mountain to gather rocks. One ambitious fellow lowered himself over the edge of a cliff to look for fossils. Unfortunately, his rope popped loose. As he fell through the air, he was surprised to see a fellow-student flying past him, going almost as fast in the opposite direction. "Hey, you know anything about rock-climbing?" he called out desperately.

"Not really," the answer floated down. "You know anything about dynamite?"

JUST AS LONG AS YOU KNOW THIS ONE IS NOT MY FAULT

I heard this story from an Army mineralogist who happened to be stationed in Anchorage in 1964. When the great earthquake hit, Joe was in his bathroom, and his first inkling of trouble came when the water in his toilet suddenly shot up seven feet and splashed all over the ceiling. Joe didn't have to think very long about the implications of this before running out of his house into the street.

By then, the earthquake was going full tilt, so to speak, and the street was full of people. One young mother, Joe's next-door neighbor, had a toddler under each arm and a terrified look on her face. She staggered up to him and cried out, "Joe, *you're* a geologist! For god's sake, *do* something!"

NOT MANY WOULD HAVE THE GRIT TO ESKER

"The Pilgrims were not the only newcomers to this spot," explained the pretty Plimouth Plantation guide. "Plymouth Rock itself is a glacial erratic, brought here from Canada only ten thousand years ago by the action of gigantic moving glaciers."

Up piped a heckler. "Gigantic moving glaciers, huh? Where are they now?"

"Oh," said the guide with a smile, "they just went back to get more rocks."

AT LEAST HE REMEMBERED THE SIGNIFICANT PART

Two honeymooners visiting New Hampshire climbed to the top of Mount Monadnock. Said the young husband, "Did you know that this peak is the lonely remnant of a massive geological upthrust eight million and three years ago?"

"Eight million and three!" marveled his wife. "How could anybody know something like that?"

"Easy," said the knowledgeable fellow. "I took geology my junior year, and back then it was only eight million."

AMY SCHOENER'S DICTIONARY OF GEOLOGY

Aa-aa: excellent Moody bond rating
Angle of repose: book by Wallace Stegner

Cinder cone: the least popular of Baskin-Robbins's thirty-one flavors
Cross-bedding: stitch used in quilting
Diorite: undertaker's promotional line for burials
Downthrusting:—expurgated
Fault: something the other party is always at
Fossils: maladies diagnosed by Dr. Foss
Groundwater: water crushed down to its components, hydrogen and oxygen
Holocene: an entire vista
Magma: a mother who incessantly mags
Mica: M. Jackson's first name, for short
Moraine: meteorological problem in western Oregon
Ondographic rhythms: background tape for break-dancing by the Ondographics
Quartz: liquid measure, two pintz
Range: where the home is on
Schist: geological curse word
Zeolite: bioluminescence attributable to microscopic zeols

Ichthyology

NO POINT IN FISHING FOR COMPLIMENTS!

This was the third dinner party where Madame LaTelle had been seated next to the famous ichthyologist, and he *still* didn't remember her name! Gently she reproached him for his forgetfulness.

"I'm terribly sorry, Madame," he responded. "But—if I remembered your name, I might forget a fish!"

AN ICHTHYOLOGIST MIGHT FORGET A FISH; A CAT WILL NOT

The great experimentalist and general trickster R. W. Wood once designed for himself an enormous spectroscopic camera, featuring a forty-two-foot-long wooden tube about six inches in diameter, with a slit at one end and a diffraction grating at the other. The camera was set up in the cow shed of his summer house on Long Island.

One spring, however, Wood returned to find that spiders had been at work during his absence, filling the tube from end to end with their webs. He dragged the tube to the lawn outside and, by fair means or foul, persuaded the family cat to climb in one end. Then Wood closed up the tube behind her and set down a fish at the other end. The cat quickly made its way down the tube to the fish, carrying with her all the spiderwebs.

FISHY BUSINESS AT HARVARD

The Swiss naturalist Louis Agassiz, most famous for pioneering the concept of an Ice Age, spent most of his working life at Harvard. While Darwin occupied himself with barnacles, Agassiz made vast collections of fish. Fishermen from all over the country were urged to send their rarest specimens to Harvard for Agassiz. One contributor wondered why: "Is it a fish shop Mr. Agassiz keeps, or a restaurant?"

Among the enthusiasts who helped Agassiz build his fish collection was Boston's famous antislavery senator, Charles Sumner. Sumner caught sight of a rare fish on ice among the stalls of teeming Quincy Market and rushed it at once to Agassiz. (Sumner, by the way, had been among the earlier, unsuccessful suitors of Agassiz's wife, Elizabeth Carey Agassiz, later to become the first president of Radcliffe.)

Other close family friends included Henry Wadsworth Longfellow and Ralph Waldo Emerson. On one occasion, Agassiz invited Longfellow to join a hunting party. Longfellow refused when he heard that Emerson would be there with a gun, declaring with unpoetic flatness that "somebody will be shot."

Agassiz liked to reminisce that during his youth he was once asked by "an estimable lady in Paris . . . how a man of sense could spend his days in dissecting a fish." His reply, recalled years later, was, "Madam, if I could live by a brook full of gudgeons, I should ask nothing better than to spend my life there."

Mathematics

HOW ABOUT YOU MAKE US SOME NICE RUSTIC TABLES?

The flood is over and the ark has landed. "Go forth and multiply," Noah tells the animals.

A few months later, he decides to take a stroll and see how the animals are doing. Everywhere he looks he finds baby animals. Everyone is doing fine except for one pair of little snakes. "Please, Noah," say the snakes, "we need you to cut down some trees for us."

"No problem," says Noah. He cuts down a few trees and goes

home scratching his head. A few weeks later he gets curious and comes back to check on the snakes. They now have lots of little snakes and everyone is happy. "What happened?" he asks them.

"We're adders," the snakes explain. "So we need logs to multiply."

MATHEMATICIAN'S NICE CLEAN LIMERICK

$$\int_{1}^{\sqrt[3]{3}} z^2 dz \times \cos\left(\frac{3 \times \pi}{9}\right) = \ln(\sqrt[3]{e})$$

TRANSLATION OF MATHEMATICIAN'S NICE CLEAN LIMERICK

Integral z-squared dz
From 1 to the cube root of three
Times the cosine
Of 3 pi over nine
Equals log of the cube root of e.

MATHEMATICIAN'S NICE LESS CLEAN LIMERICK

There once was a mathematician
Who preferred an exotic position.
'Twas the joy of his life
To achieve with his wife
Topologically complex coition.

MATHEMATICIAN'S FAREWELL LIMERICK

A mathematician of Trinity
Was computing the cube of infinity
But the number of digits
Soon gave him such fidgets
He dropped it and took up divinity.

MATHEMATICIAN'S NIGHTMARE LIBRARY

First Aid for Dedekind Cuts
Jacobeans and their Struggle for Independence
An Unabridged List of the Even Primes
22/7: The First 1000 Digits

Story said to be true: In the great Strand second-hand bookstore of New York, you can find *Surgery on Manifolds* in the medical section.

FROM THE GREETING CARD SECTION OF THE MATHEMATICIAN'S
NIGHTMARE BOOKSTORE
> *Sorry I reformatted your disk!*
> *So—you were denied tenure.*
> *Thank you for your flawed proof of my theorem.*
> *Happy 1011001th birthday!*
> *And you thought Hilbert had problems?*

AND FROM THEIR RACK OF BUMPER STICKERS
> *Mathematicians have extended functions.*
> *A good mathematician can make a finite difference.*
> *Math and alcohol don't mix—never drink and derive.*

---

and the question is:
Why is 1/z like the Catholic Church?

and the answer is:
Both have a simple Pole at the center.

SOME DAY BILLY WILL TELL ALL THIS TO HIS ANALYST
The first-grade teacher asked the children to tell what their parents did for a living. Everyone but Billy had an answer. Billy didn't know, so he went home that night with instructions to find out. Next day, the teacher said, "Now, Billy, did you ask your parents what they do?"

"Yes, and my mom sent you a note."

"That's nice, Billy. While I'm looking at the note, you can tell the class yourself."

Billy turned to the class and said proudly, "My parents told me they run a great big whorehouse."

The teacher, nearly fainting with horror, read the note, which said, "Actually, my husband and I are research mathematicians. What we do at work, a six-year-old could *never* understand."

BOURBAKI IN THE ELEMENTARY GRADES
André Weil, who vehemently denies that Bourbaki can be blamed for the so-called New Math, has a daughter the right age to have been hit with it quite young. And when she learned the symbol in her schoolbook for the empty set—a Norwegian "ø"—had been introduced by her own father, she was clearly impressed.

Next day at dinner, she remarked, "Do you know, I felt so proud today telling the class that my father invented the empty set!"

READY, SET, STAND UP!

In the same era, another mathematician's son came home and announced that his class was learning set theory. "For instance," said the little boy, "the teacher asked everyone who had eggs for breakfast to stand up. Then that was the set of people who had eggs for breakfast. Then she asked everyone who had cereal for breakfast to stand up. That was the set of people who had cereal for breakfast. Then she asked for people who had nothing for breakfast to stand up. No one stood up, so that was the empty set."

"I see," said the mathematician. "So, these carrots on my plate—could they be a set?"

The little boy was clearly troubled by the question. "Well," he said slowly, "if the carrots could stand up . . ."

NO, GO FISH—MATHEMATICALLY SPEAKING

One cold, rainy evening, two mathematicians were sitting around the fireplace swapping jokes and puzzles. "Two fishermen were comparing their catch," said one fellow. "The first fisherman said, 'I have two fish.' The second fisherman said, 'Well, if I squared the number of fish I have, and subtracted from that the number of fish I have, I'd end up with two also.' So, how many fish did the second fisherman have?"

Without hesitation, his friend replied, "Minus one fish."

LET Y = NUMBER OF X IT TAKES TO CHANGE A LIGHT BULB

x	y
Real functions	None, it's too complex for them.
Numerical analysts	0.99987, after four iterations.
Statisticians	One, with .95% confidence—or, one, on the average.
Constructive mathematicians	None. They do not believe in infinitesimal rotations.
Number theorists	Only one, but the margin is too small for a proof.
Classical geometers	None. It cannot be done with a straightedge and compass.

WORLD'S MOST SELF-REFERENTIAL LIGHT BULB JOKES

How many light bulbs does it take to change a light bulb?
One, if it knows its own Gödel number.

How many light bulb jokes does it take to change a
light bulb joke?
*The probability that a given light bulb joke will be submitted
in any given week is .4, and the probability that it will
have changed
detectably since the last transmission is .2.
Hence, assuming independence (which is reasonable
since no submitter of a light bulb joke ever seems to know
it has been submitted before, within the last two or three weeks),
the probability that it will change in a given week is .08.
So it takes about 12.5 light bulb jokes to change a light bulb joke.*

WORLD'S DARKEST LIGHT BULB JOKE

How many survivors of nuclear war does it take to change
a light bulb?
So who needs light bulbs when you already glow in the dark?

TAKE A PARTIAL DERIVATIVE OF COFFEA ARABICA . . .

According to Paul Erdös, a mathematician is a device for turning coffee into theorems.

UNPOPULAR SCIENCE

Christopher Clavius (1537–1612), a mathematician from whose textbooks Descartes studied, revised the Julian calendar at the request of Pope Gregory XIII. In order to synchronize calendar dates with the sun, the Gregorian calendar decreed that October 4, 1582 was to be followed immediately by October 15, 1582. Riots swept over Europe, protesting this wicked plot by mathematicians—to rob the honest citizenry of ten whole days!

NEW INSIGHT, PLUS OR MINUS ONE

$$-1 = -1$$
$$-1/1 = -1/1$$
$$-1/1 = 1/-1$$
$$\text{square root of } (-1/1) = \text{square root of } (1/-1)$$
$$(\text{square root of } -1)/1 = 1/(\text{square root of } -1)$$
$$i/1 = 1/i$$
$$i = 1/i$$
$$i * i = 1$$
$$-1 = 1$$

---

and the question is:

What do you get if you cross a tsetse fly with a mountain climber?

and the answer is:

Nothing. You can't cross a vector with a scalar.

PROOF THAT 2 = 1

$$\text{Let } x = y.$$
$$\text{Then } x^2 = xy,$$
$$\text{so } x^2 - y^2 = xy - y^2,$$
or, in other words, $(x+y)(x-y) = y(x-y)$.
Canceling yields $x+y = y$, hence $2y = y$ and $2 = 1$.

SEQUITUR—A PROOF THAT I AM POPE

Clearly the Pope and I are two.
But we have just shown that $2 = 1$.
Therefore the Pope and I are one.

PURE JINGOISM

A mathematician noted for his championship of pure (as opposed to applied) mathematics was once asked if he thought there was really any conflict between the two fields.

His reply: "Conflict? Nonsense! The two have no point of contact whatsoever."

---

and the question is:
2b or not 2b, that is the question.

and the answer is:
No, "2b or not 2b" is the *answer*.
The question is, what is the square root of $4b^2$?

MATHEMATICAL TOMBSTONE TERRITORY
Here lies Isaac Newton—A body at rest tends to remain at rest.
Here lies David Hilbert—He no longer has problems.
Euclid—his spirit is gone but here lie his elements.
Here lies Heisenberg—Maybe!
R.I.P. Henri Lebesgue—Talent beyond measure.
Here lies G. H. Hardy with no apologies.
Here lies S. Banach with plenty of space.
Final resting place of Georg Cantor for the next $\aleph_0$ years.
Here lies Pierre de Fermat—Unfortunately this stone is too small to contain a proper epitaph.

Oceanography

DEEP THINKER

Two oceanography students from the great midwestern plains embarked on their first research voyage. As they stood gazing over the rail at the wide expanse of Pacific blue, one of them whistled. "I never saw that much water before in my life. How about you?"

The other preferred to look blasé. "Huh, that's nothing. All you can see from here's the *top!*"

IN WHICH CASE IT WOULD BE SHOWN TO BE THE DUMB BELL

Two teams of marine biologists went down to the ocean floor. We won't tell you their nationalities; let's just call them the smart team and the stupid team. The stupid team noticed that someone had lowered a diving bell nearby. The problem was, which team did the diving bell belong to?

Fortunately the captain of the stupid team was able to figure out a way to get the answer. All he had to do was to swim over to the diving bell and knock at the window. If the people inside were from his own country, they would immediately open it.

Physics

GETTING PHYSICAL WITH A LIGHT BULB

How many high-energy experimentalists does it take to change a light bulb?

Two hundred, 136 to smash it to subatomic fragments and 64 to analyze them.

How many high-energy theorists does it take to change a light bulb?

Sorry—would you repeat the question?

GENERAL BENEFITS AND SPECIAL DANGERS OF RELATIVITY

There was a bold pilot named Bright
Whose plane was much faster than light.
So he took off one day
In a relative way
And returned on the previous night.

There was a young fellow named Fiske
Whose stroke was excessively brisk.
So fast was his action
The Lorentz contraction
Diminished his dong to a disk.

SCIENCE, SCHMIENCE, LET'S MAKE SOME MONEY!

A famous physicist had been approached to write a book on his work. After drafting a few sample chapters and an outline, he brought the project to his agent. The agent claimed to love the work so far—all but the title.

"Maybe *Elementary Particle Physics* sounds a bit too heavy," the physicist admitted.

"No, baby, no!" his agent cried. "Real science is big bucks

nowadays! I can guarantee twice the money if you just get rid of the word 'elementary'!"

Plant Science

WELL WHAT I SAY IS, NUTS TO THEM!

Plant hybridizer Luther Burbank (1849–1926) created many new varieties of plants, but not all his novelties were successes. One notable failure was a walnut that could be cracked easily by hand. It isn't that Burbank couldn't get trees to produce a nut with a paper-thin shell, or that consumers weren't eager to buy them. But, unfortunately, there is no way for growers to keep the birds and squirrels from eating them just as fast as they develop!

THUS ENDING THE BRAGGING ABOUT HER FLOWERS

William Lawrence Bragg (1890–1971), at twenty-five the youngest person ever to win the Nobel Prize in physics, was an avid amateur gardener. When he moved to London to head the Royal Institution, he reluctantly left behind the beautiful Cambridge garden he had spent so many years perfecting. Life in a city apartment made him restless and unhappy until he found an ingenious solution to his problem.

Dressed in old gardening clothes with a spade over one shoulder, he patrolled the streets of a nearby wealthy district until he found a house whose garden tempted him. Then he rang the bell and, tipping his hat respectfully to the lady of the house, introduced himself as "Willie," an odd-job gardener with one free afternoon a week. His employer found Willie an absolute treasure.

Until, alas, one day a knowledgeable visitor looked out through her window and gasped, "Good heavens, what is Sir Lawrence Bragg doing in your garden?"

RUTHERFORD ENDS HIS EARLY SPADE-WORK

The great experimental physicist Sir Ernest Rutherford (1871–1937) was a native New Zealander with none of Bragg's English enthusiasm for flowers. Maybe he got enough of gardening in his youth. Legend has it he was spading up the family vegetable plot when word arrived that he had received a long-awaited scholarship to Cambridge. Rutherford threw down his shovel and cried, "That's the last potato I'll dig!"

MOST FAMOUS SENTENCE CONTAINING THE WORD "HORTICUL-
TURE"

You can lead a horticulture but you cannot make her think.

Social Science*

ON SOCIAL SCIENCE THEORIES

By the time a social science theory is formulated in such a way that it can be tested, changing circumstances have already made it obsolete.

ON THE NUMBER AND COMPLEXITY OF VARIABLES

One approaches any given problem with the belief that it consists of about a dozen variables of which—with intelligence and goodwill—two-thirds or three-quarters can be brought under control. One ends up by realizing that, in fact, the number of variables is over a hundred, and that, at best, three or four can be controlled.

ON ECONOMIC THEORY

Economic theorists start with untenable assumptions (e.g., that a man's earnings equal the value of his marginal product) and proceed by impeccable reasoning (including most rigorous mathematics) to incredible conclusions (e.g., that a man's earnings equal the value of his marginal product).

ON EXPECTATIONS AND ACHIEVEMENTS

In the most favorable circumstances, achievements cannot exceed the square root of expectations.

ON CONSUMPTION PATTERNS

Other people's patterns of expenditure and consumption are highly irrational and slightly immoral.

THE ISSAWI-WILCOX PRINCIPLE

Problems increase in geometric ratio, solutions in arithmetic ratio.

* These jokes are reprinted with permission from the new enlarged edition of *Issawi's Laws of Social Motion* by Charles Issawi (Princeton, NJ: The Darwin Press, (1973); 1991.)

ON PREDICTION

If you predict the worst possible outcome of any situation, the probability of your being right is 0.9135.

ON SOLVERS OF MIDDLE-EASTERN PROBLEMS

God sent Moses, and he couldn't fix it; he sent Jesus, and he couldn't fix it; he sent Muhammad, and he couldn't fix it. Do you think you can fix it?

Statistics

YOU COULD CALL THIS A MEAN STORY

Three statisticians went deer-hunting with bows and arrows. They crept through the forest until they spotted a magnificent buck. The first statistician shot, and his arrow landed five meters to the right of the deer. The second one shot, and her arrow landed five meters to the left of it. So the third one jumped out of the bushes and shouted, "We got him! We got him!"

HOW ABOUT TWO BOMBS AND A MANIAC ROBOT?

Then there was the statistician who hated to fly because he had nightmares about terrorists with bombs. Yes, he knew it was a million to one chance, but that wasn't good enough. So he took a lot of trains until he realized what he had to do.

Now whenever he flies, he packs a bomb in his own suitcase. Hey, do you know what the odds are against an airplane carrying *two* bombs?

MOST STATISTICALLY SIGNIFICANT FACT WE KNOW

96.37% of All Statistics Are Made Up.

Interdisciplinary Studies

BUT WHY WERE THEY ALL SO EAGER TO CLAIM MEMBERSHIP IN THE OLDEST PROFESSION?

A doctor, an engineer, and a dean were arguing over which was the oldest profession.

"Eve was taken out of Adam's rib," said the doctor. "Clearly a surgical operation."

The engineer protested. "Before God even got around to Adam and Eve, He had to bring order out of chaos—that's an engineering job."

"Aha!" said the dean. "And who created the chaos?"

WHO SAYS THAT THERE'S NO ACCOUNTING FOR TASTES?

A mathematician, an engineer, and an accountant were chatting when a kid came by looking for the answer to a homework problem: What is the square root of four?

"Are we talking integers here, or natural numbers?" asked the mathematician. The kid looked blank. "Okay, never mind. It's plus two or minus two."

"I can make that considerably more precise," said the engineer, whipping out a calculator. "It's 1.99762, correct to four decimal places."

"You two are forgetting the most important thing," said the accountant, giving the kid a penetrating look. "Tell me—what do you *want* the square root of four to be?"

ROCK MUSIC: NOT JUST FOR GEOLOGISTS

The radiologists' theme song: "I'm Looking Through You."

The sewage-treatment engineers' theme song: "Love That Dirty Water."

Songs NASA scientists always want to hear: "Up, Up and Away," "Rocket Man," and "Don't Bring Me Down."

Tunes for a science major up all night for finals: "Hard Day's Night," "Don't Know Much about History," and "Don't Let the Sun Catch You Crying."

For mineralogists: "Rock Around the Clock" as performed by the Rolling Stones.
For astronomers: "Starry, Starry Night" as performed by Bill Haley and the Comets.
For aeronautical engineers: "Fly Away with Me" as performed by Jefferson Airplane.

WHEN YOU HEAR THERE'S NOTHING TO WORRY ABOUT, THAT'S WHEN YOU *REALLY* START TO WORRY

A group of investors decided that horse-racing could be made to pay on a scientific basis. So, they hired a team of biologists, a team of physicists, and a team of mathematicians to spend a year studying the question. At the end of the year, all three teams announced complete solutions. The investors decided to celebrate with a gala dinner where all three plans could be unveiled.

The mathematicians had the thickest report, so the chief mathematician was asked to give the first talk: "Ladies and gentlemen, you have nothing to worry about. Without describing the many details of our proof, we can guarantee a solution to the problem you gave us—it turns out that every race is won by a least one horse. But we have been able to go beyond even this, and can show that the solution is unique: every race is won by no more than one horse!"

The biologists, who had spent the most money, went next. They were also able to show that the investors had nothing to worry about. By using the latest technology of genetic engineering, the biologists could easily set up a breeding program to produce an unbeatable racehorse, at a cost well below a million a year, in about two hundred years.

Now the investors' hopes were riding on the physicists. The chief physicist also began by assuring them that their troubles were over. "We have perfected a method for predicting with 96 percent certainty the winner of any given race. The method is based on a very few simplifying assumptions. First, let each horse be a perfect rolling sphere . . ."

DON'T CALL THEM, THEY'LL CALL YOU

Ask a theoretical physicist his phone number, and he'll tell you it's a trivial consequence of Maxwell's equations.

Ask a mathematician his phone number, and he'll tell you it's a trivial consequence of Maxwell's equations with the appropriate boundary conditions.

Ask an experimental physicist his phone number, and he'll tell you that so far he knows it to only four significant figures.

Ask an astrophysicist his phone number, and he'll tell you that it's on the order of ten to the sixth.

Ask a computer scientist his phone number, and he'll offer to sell you a program that will try every telephone until you find his.

Ask an economist his phone number, and he'll want to know what it's worth to you.

Ask a demographer his phone number, and he'll tell you not only the number but the first three decimal places thereafter.

INFALLIBLE SELF-KNOWLEDGE

Biologists think they're biochemists,
Biochemists think they're chemists,
Chemists think they're physical chemists,
Physical chemists think they're physicists,
Physicists think they're gods,
And God thinks he's a mathematician.

BUT LATER HIS INTEREST IN OTHER METHODS COMPOUNDED DAILY

A physicist, an engineer, and an economist were stranded on a desert island with nothing to eat but three cans of tuna. The physicist got hungry first, so he constructed a huge mirror that focused the sun's rays on top of the can. Soon the can got so hot that it exploded, scattering fragments of tuna everywhere.

The engineer bent down a palm tree to make a catapult, which smashed his can into the side of a cliff so hard that it split in half, dumping its contents onto the rocks below.

The economist said, "Assume a can opener."

A COFFEEPOT WOULD HAVE BEEN EMPTIED EVEN FASTER

A physicist and a mathematician were being tested for their ability to perform simple tasks.

"Now," said the examiner to the physicist, handing her an empty teakettle, "suppose you want to boil some water. You can use any of the equipment in this kitchen. How do you proceed?"

With a shrug, the physicist went to the sink, poured water into the kettle, walked to the stove, turned on a burner, and put the kettle on the burner.

"Good. You pass," said the examiner. He turned off the burner, and passed the kettle to the mathematician saying, "What about you?"

The mathematician carried the kettle to the sink and emptied it down the drain. "This reduces to a problem already solved."

IN SHORT, IT'S KIND OF WORKING ON AND OFF

"I don't think my directional signal is working," a physicist complained to her friend the mathematician. "Would you mind getting out of the car to take a look?"

The mathematician walked over behind the car. "Okay, turn the blinker on. Yes, it's working; now it isn't, now it is, now it isn't . . ."

SIGNS OF A MISMATCH: ACCORDING TO C. N. YANG, THIS ILLUS-
TRATES THE DIFFERENCE BETWEEN MATHEMATICS AND PHYSICS

We first came across this story in Stan Ulam's wonderful autobiography, *Adventures of a Mathematician*: A tourist with a bundle of
dirty shirts under his arm was searching the streets of a strange city
for a laundry. Finally he saw a sign in a window: "LAUNDRY TAKEN
IN HERE." He rushed into the shop and dumped his shirts on the
counter, to the consternation of the woman behind it.

"What is this?" she protested. "We don't do laundry here!"

"You don't? But what about that sign in your window that says
'LAUNDRY TAKEN IN HERE'?"

"That is our window, and that is our sign. But here we do not do
laundry. Here, we make signs."

---

*"There are only two kinds of modern mathematics books—those you
cannot read beyond the first page and those you cannot read beyond the
first sentence."*

C. N. YANG, *1957* NOBEL LAUREATE IN PHYSICS

THE LOGIC OF EVEN WOOLLY THINKING

A train was chugging through the Swiss countryside. A physicist,
a philosopher, and a mathematician were sharing a compartment.
After passing about the seventh mountain shepherd with his flock, the
physicist said, "It looks as if all the sheep in this canton are white."

"Not proven," demurred the logician, "though we could conclude
that *some* of the sheep in this canton are white."

The mathematician shook her head. "So far as I can see, some
sheep in this canton are white on one side."

BUT IT WAS A BAD IDEA TO LET THE PHYSICIST DEMONSTRATE
UNIQUENESS

A physicist and a mathematician took adjoining rooms in a hotel.
At midnight, the loud buzzing of a fire alarm woke everyone. The
physicist got his shoes on first, and peered into the corridor. It was a
little smoky, but the fire exit was easy to locate and the physicist
headed for it.

The mathematician also proceeded to the fire exit. He opened it,
and looked down the fire escape. Clearly, it would be easy to follow
the physicist down to the ground. A solution, therefore, could be seen

to exist. Satisfied, the mathematician returned to his room and fell asleep.

CURVACEOUS BUT VEXATIOUS

Mathematicians have little patience with the ways physicists torment equations to fit reality. John von Neumann once endured a physics lecture on fitting some experimental points to a predicted mathematical curve. It was clear from the lecturer's slides that in fact the points were very scattered. Von Neumann leaned over and whispered to his neighbor, "At least the points lie on a plane."

THE PHYSICIST'S PROOF THAT 2 × 2 = 3

$$2 \times 2 = 2 \times (1/(\tfrac{1}{2})) =$$
$$2 \times (1/(1-\tfrac{1}{2})) =$$
$$2 \times (1 + \tfrac{1}{2} + (\tfrac{1}{2})^2 + (\tfrac{1}{2})^3 + \ldots) =$$
$$\text{(to first order) } 2 \times (1 + \tfrac{1}{2}) = 3$$

KAC 22

The mathematician Mark Kac was giving a seminar at Caltech to an audience that included the irrepressible physicist R. P. Feynman. Feynman loved to take potshots at what he considered the petty attachments to rigor of mathematicians, and when Kac paused for breath Feynman grabbed his chance. "If mathematics did not exist," Feynman announced, "it would set the world back one week."

Without hesitation Kac replied, "Precisely the week in which God *created* the world."

WELL, THEY'RE LUCKY THE MATHEMATICIAN WASN'T DIRAC

At one very fancy conference, the participants got the chance to go up in hot air balloons. Two physicists trying it for the first time got caught in a high-level breeze and were blown far from their starting-point. Finally they spotted a solitary hiker. "Halloo!" they cried. "Can you tell us where we are?"

The hiker looked up, but waited until they were almost out of earshot before shouting back, "You're in a balloon!"

"Damn!" said one physicist. "Just our luck to run into a mathematician."

"A mathematician? How could you tell?"

"Couldn't you? Look, his answer was completely correct. Then, he took a long time to produce it. And nevertheless it was totally useless."

A COMPOSITE OF PROOFS THAT ALL ODD NUMBERS ARE PRIME.
The mathematician's proof:
3 is prime,
5 is prime,
7 is prime,
and the rest by induction.
The physicist's proof:
3 is prime,
5 is prime,
7 is prime,
(9, experimental error),
11 is prime, . . .
The engineer's proof:
3 is prime,
5 is prime,
7 is prime,
9 is something you can build around, . . .
The philosopher's proof:
3 is prime,
5 is prime,
7 is prime,
9 is a matter of definition, . . .
The theologian's proof:
1 is prime,
3 is prime,
any other numbers are irrelevant.
The social scientist's proof:
3 is prime,
5 is prime,
7 is prime,
9 is prime, . . .
Some computer scientists were able to generate this proof:
3 is prime,
3 is prime,
3 is prime, . . .
And let's not forget the English major's proof that
all odd numbers are prime:
1 is prime,
2 is prime,
3 is prime,
4 is prime, . . .

FERMAT'S MARGINAL PROOF THAT ALL PRIME NUMBERS ARE ODD

$4n + 1$ is odd, $4n + 3$ is odd—*but*, you say, what about 2?
Ah, 2 is the oddest prime of them all, and the proof is complete.

Death and the Scientist

AVOIDING THE TURN OF THE SKEW

A mathematician and a biologist were sharing a cell the night before their execution (for crimes unimaginable). The executioner came to ask for their last wishes.

The mathematician glanced at the biologist and said, "I've been doing some work in mathematical biology, and I've got some interesting results. Before I die, would you arrange for me to give a seminar on my work?"

"Sure," said the executioner, and turned to the biologist. "Now, what would you like?"

The biologist said, "I would like to be executed before the seminar."

AND IF HE WANTED TO GET ELECTROCUTED, HE COULD HAVE MAJORED IN ELECTRICAL ENGINEERING

A biologist and an engineer were sentenced to be executed. They took the biologist first. "You get a choice," the warden told him. "What'll it be—the firing squad or the electric chair?"

The biologist turned pale. "If I could stand blood, I would have gone to med school," he said. "I'll take the chair." They strapped him in and pulled the switch—nothing happened. "Okay," said the warden, with a shrug. "I guess I have to pardon you." So they sent the biologist back to the cell, where he quickly told the engineer what had happened.

Then the death squad arrived for the engineer. "What do you choose?" they asked. "Shooting or the chair?"

The engineer gave them a scornful look. "Shooting, of course. It's clear your *chair* doesn't work."

SO THEY GAVE HIM A CONSULTING FEE AND *THEN* THEY CHOPPED HIS HEAD OFF

Not long after the fall of the Bastille, the French mobs were getting tired of aristocrats, so they started chopping off the heads of the Académie. An astronomer, a mathematician, and an engineer found themselves together at the scaffold.

"Do you have any last request?" the headsman asked the astronomer.

"Yes," said the astronomer. "If I must put my head on the block, I would like to do so with my face turned toward the stars."

So they arranged the block so that he could lie down on his back facing the stars—and the guillotine, which descended with a deadly hiss. But for some reason, the blade stopped a good two inches above his neck. The crowd roared that after this miracle the astronomer should be set free, and the executioner released him.

The next on the block was the mathematician. "Do you want to lie on your back too?" asked the executioner.

"Of course," said the mathematician. "It's important to duplicate the previous conditions."

Once again the guillotine hissed into action, once again the blade came short. The mathematician too was released at the crowd's insistence.

Then came the engineer. Without even asking him his preference, the frustrated executioner pushed him under the blade, and then left him lying there looking up while his assistants checked the mechanism. Finding nothing, they were just about to try once more when the engineer cried out, "Wait! I see it! Your rope gets caught in the top left pulley."

THIS PLAN COULD HAVE BEEN BETTER EXECUTED

An engineer and a physicist, both sentenced to be shot at dawn, were sharing a cell. Fortunately, they came up with a plan. As the revolutionaries led the physicist out into the cold gray light of morning, the engineer set fire to a small pile of straw on the window-ledge of their cell. It quickly blazed up.

"Look!" the physicist shouted to his captors. "The cell-block is burning!" The soldiers dropped their guns and raced to put out the fire. Furthermore, the warden decided that the physicist should receive a pardon.

Now the squad returned for the engineer. As you might expect, the physicist found it a little harder to get a fire going. In fact, the engineer was already looking down the rifle barrels of the assembled squad when he finally saw the little thread of smoke that could mean his freedom. So as fast as he could, the engineer shouted, "Fire!"

Love, Sex, Marriage, and Scientists

Sex is a Sublimation of the Mathematical Drive

HIS TELLTALE SLEEVE

A physicist took the day off from the accelerator at CERN to do some shopping with his wife in Geneva. At ten o'clock, she was to get her hair cut. "Now, don't wander off," she admonished her husband. "I'll be finished in an hour, and when I am I want to find you right here with the car."

The physicist was sitting in the front seat reading Feynman when a beautiful young woman tapped on his window. Her car had a flat tire, and she owned no jack. Could he help?

He could, but in the process he got quite dirty. Fortunately the young woman's apartment was nearby, so she invited him up to wash his hands.

Soon, however, one thing led to another. Two hours later the conscience-stricken physicist looked at his watch, which was all he happened to be wearing at the moment, and leaped to his feet. As he struggled into his clothes, an idea came to him.

"I'm doomed unless—do you have any flour here?"

"But, of course I have flour."

"Good, I need some. Ah, now sprinkle a bit of it over my jacket—especially the sleeves—wonderful!" Then he sprinted out the door.

His angry wife was waiting by the beauty parlor. "Listen, darling," he said, "Let me explain—I'm terribly sorry. You see, a young woman asked me to help her change her tire. What could I say? Then she invited me to her apartment to wash up. Before I knew what had happened we were rolling around on the floor making passionate love—"

"You liar!" cried his wife. "You utter sneak! You stand there, with chalk dust all over you, trying to tell me you didn't go back to CERN to do *physics!*"

WHEREAS A MATHEMATICIAN WOULD HAVE SAVED HIMSELF A LOT OF TROUBLE BY ASKING ABOUT FERMAT'S LAST THEOREM

A man found a bottle washed up on the seashore. He opened it, and a genie appeared. "Very well, Master," said the genie. "Tell me your third and final wish?"

"My third wish? What do you mean? I haven't had any wishes yet."

"It is natural that you should forget," said the genie. "You see, your *second* wish was that everything would be put back as it was before your first wish. In any case, you have one remaining wish."

"One wish? Only one?" said the man. "Then I think that I shall wish to be irresistible to women."

"Very well, Master," said the genie, waving his wand. "Strange— that was your first wish as well."

TITLE TITILLATION

A West Coast mathematician hinted to colleagues that he had some interesting results to report, but he was surprised when more than a hundred people showed up to hear him lecture on convex sets and inequalities.

Later he found out that the university bulletin had announced his title as "Convicts, Sex, and Inequality."

HE DID SEEM TO HAVE SOME KIND OF DEFICIT

An accountant was somehow persuaded to go to his fortieth college reunion. "Jimmy, old boy, good to see you!" said the class president, pumping his hand up and down. "Have a cigar?"

"No thanks," said the accountant politely. "I tried smoking one once, but I didn't like it."

"Never mind the cigar then—let me get you a beer."

"Thanks, no. I did try drinking once, but I just didn't care for it."

"How about some poker then? A few of the fellows are getting together in my room later on . . ."

"Thanks, but I'll pass. I tried gambling once, but it didn't suit me. My son might show up later, maybe he'll join you."

"Your son? He must be an *only* child?"

I LIKE THE ONE THAT'S EASY TO DO IN YOUR HEAD

MATH TEACHER: Sex is like differential geometry. When it's good, it's very, very good. When it's bad it's still pretty good.

STUDENT: Sex is pretty good. When it's good, it's very, very good. When it's bad, it's like differential geometry.

ARTISTIC LICENSE*

> *While Titian was mixing his madder,*
> *His model ascended a ladder.*
> *Her position, to Titian,*
> *Suggested coition,*
> *So he climbed up the ladder and had 'er.*

WHAT'S YOUR ADDRESS? I'LL SEND YOU ALL MY PREPRINTS!

An elderly botanist crowned his life work by producing a beautiful monograph on the subject of buttercups. So outstanding was his book that Mother Nature herself took notice. Materializing between his microscope and his microtome, she announced, "My son, your great work on buttercups has pleased me so deeply I want to reward you. For the rest of your life whenever you wish for butter it will appear. All the butter you want, indeed, all the dairy products of every kind, will be yours with no exertion on your part."

The botanist stammered out thanks as best he could. But Mother Nature could see that the eyes behind his bifocals were filled with sorrow. "What is it, my child?" she asked. "Surely my gift should bring you joy?"

"Oh, yes, ma'am, it does, it does. I just can't help thinking how things might have turned out if I'd stuck with my original thesis topic—the pussywillow."

I WASN'T INVOLVED IN THAT KIND OF A CONFERENCE

Yet another international conference story: the American scientist in Paris, out for a predawn run in the Bois de Boulogne. This morning he was trying to work off some rich French sauces from last night's

---

* Said to be John von Neumann's favorite limerick

banquet. Not satisfied with jogging his usual mile or so, he found a nice grassy spot and began to do some push-ups.

A passing gendarme regarded him with curiosity, then with growing comprehension. Approaching the athlete, he discreetly whispered, "Monsieur, Madame has departed."

BUT THE FRENCH UNDERSTAND THE LOGIC OF THESE THINGS
(SAID TO BE A VON NEUMANN FAVORITE)
In America: Everything is permitted that is not explicitly forbidden.
In Germany: Everything is forbidden that is not explicitly permitted.
In France: Everything is permitted that is explicitly forbidden.

KIND OF REMINDS ME OF A CERTAIN FRENCH
INSTITUTE MEMBER
One swashbuckling mathematician evoked the comment, "Since he came to Berkeley he's had at least six wives—have to admit, three of them were his own."

BESIDES, MY HUSBAND DOESN'T SPEAK MUCH FRENCH
"There is one thing, doctor," said the young mother-to-be. "When the baby is born, does my husband have to be there?"

The obstetrician was puzzled. "Surely you want to share this experience with the father of your child?"

"Oh, absolutely. But he and my husband just don't get along."

GIVING A WHOLE NEW MEANING TO "THAT WAS NO LADY . . ."
One of Dirac's innovations in quantum mechanics involved splitting mathematical brackets into two symmetric halves he called the "ket" and the "bra." When I first heard this, I assumed it was with a certain otherworldly innocence that he had introduced ladies' underwear into mathematical physics. Now I'm not so sure. Along with his fondness for abstract symmetry he also had a taste for mildly salacious humor, both of which show up in the following joke he liked to tell:

"When a man says yes he means perhaps, when he says perhaps he means no, when he says no he is no diplomat. When a lady says no she means perhaps, when she says perhaps she means yes, when she says yes she is no lady."

Another of Dirac's favorite jokes goes as follows:

The new young priest had been invited for dinner by one of his parishioners, and noticed with approval that there were many little children seated around the table.

"Yes, Father, we have ten," the husband said proudly. "And what is a bit remarkable is that in fact they are five sets of twins."

"Amazing!" said the priest. "Do you mean to tell me that you have had twins every time?"

"Not really, Father," said the wife with a blush. "Quite often we had nothing."

---

and the answer is:
El*lip*tical.

and the question is:
How would a mathematician analyze a kiss?

---

and the question is:
Why are a woman's breasts like computer games?

and the answer is:
They are intended for children,
but the fathers end up playing with them

CITY COLLEGE SAVED FROM WICKED EARL

In 1940, Bertrand Russell was offered a professorship at New York's City College. Unfortunately, the radical views he had expressed in his book *Marriage and Morals* were considered so shocking that a citizen's campaign was mounted to block the appointment.

In vain did H. L. Mencken defend Russell's opinions: "In one of his books he speaks favorably of adultery, but he does so in the scientific way in which one might say a word for the method of least squares, the hookworm, or a respectable volcano."

Russell's opponents took their case to the State Supreme Court, producing a brief that denounced the mathematician as "lecherous, libidinous, lustful, venerous, erotomaniac, aphrodisiac, irreverent, narrow-minded, untruthful, and bereft of moral fibre."

Although he lost the case, the aging Russell was delighted to have been described as "aphrodisiac." "I cannot think of any predecessors," he claimed, "except Apuleius and Othello."

D. H. Lawrence's long-ago verdict was less flattering. His reaction to the youthful mathematician in a bathing suit: "Poor Bertie Russell! He is all Disembodied Mind!"

YOU DON'T WANT TO BE RUNNING AROUND WITH SUNBURNED BUNSENS

Over the loudspeaker at the chemistry department pool party:
Will the gentleman with the blue and green bathing trunks please return to the men's locker room immediately. *You forgot to put them on.*

I DON'T RECOGNIZE HIM EITHER, BUT SOMETHING ABOUT HIM REMINDS ME OF THE MAN WITH THE BLUE AND GREEN BATHING TRUNKS

Three women whose husbands were teaching in the same summer school went for a stroll. Not far from their hotel, they came across a naked man sunbathing. He had fallen asleep with his towel across his face. The women moved quietly away, and one of them said to the others, "I don't know who that is, but it's certainly not *my* husband."

The second one said, "You're right, that isn't your husband."

The third said indignantly, "He's not even a member of the school!"

MATERIAL EVIDENCE

The saleswoman was baffled by her customer's request. "You don't need fifteen yards of lace to make a negligee," she insisted. "It takes only one or two."

The customer shook her head. "You don't understand—I'm marrying an experimental physicist. With them the search is always much more exciting than the discovery!"

DENDROCHRONOLOGY IN THE AMERICAN BEDROOM

"You know," the botanist's new wife confided tearfully, "when Bill wanted to spend our honeymoon looking at redwoods, maybe I should have started to worry right then. But the worst was when we got to our hotel room. The phone started to ring . . ."

"Yes?"

"And I reached over to answer it, and he wouldn't let me."

"Yes? He sounds romantic."

The bride shook her head. "He was counting its rings."

TO A PROGRAMMER, SOFTWARE IS JUST MORE FUN THAN HARDWARE

Three women were arguing the relative merits of lovers versus husbands.

The doctor spoke first. "A husband is better," she said. "If you consider all the benefits of stability and a peaceful home life, no other choice seems possible."

"A lover is better," said the lawyer. "Marriage is all very well for a year, maybe ten, even twenty. But when it stops working—think of the paperwork!"

The third was a programmer. "Having both is better," she said. "After all, a lover can hardly expect you to spend all your time with him when you have a husband. And your husband, if you tell him you're busy, doesn't want to make a fuss in case you're with your lover. So between the two, I can spend almost every night at my computer!"

SOME KINDLY STATISTICIAN SHOULD WARN THAT DOCTOR

Statistically speaking, marriages contracted in June have a high probability of ending in divorce. Other months with this property are

July, August, September, October, November, December, January, February, March, April, and May.

IF ONE IS STANDARD, THE OTHER *MUST* BE A DEVIATION

Statistics show that marriage is 83 percent effective in preventing suicide. On the other hand, statistics also show that suicide is 100 percent effective in preventing marriage.

TALES OF THE GREAT SCIENTISTS

LET'S HOPE HIS SELF-CRITICISM WAS AS GENTLE

The great Danish physicist Niels Bohr (1885–1962) was fated to be a theorist. His lab instructors claimed they had never seen a student whose bill for broken glassware came close to his, and one day when a violent explosion rocked the University of Copenhagen everyone's first thought was, "Oh, that must be Bohr."

Otto Robert Frisch recalls one day Bohr visited a lab where experimentalists were looking for new radioactive elements, using special thin-walled counters so flimsy they could barely support the normal pressure of air. Eager to show his interest in their work, Bohr reached out and grabbed one, which crumpled at his touch.

Lecturing was another of Bohr's not-very-strong points. His voice was very soft and difficult to hear past the first row. Some professors can compensate by writing a great deal on the board—but Bohr's penmanship made this a dubious addition to his talk. According to Abram Pais, who was a witness, Bohr once announced his intention to talk about "harmony," a word he reproduced on the blackboard as follows:

Then, after a few moments, he decided that a better word for his topic would be "uniformity." He returned to the board, and converted "harmony" to "uniformity" with the addition of a single dot:

Pais describes it as "the most remarkable act of calligraphy I shall ever witness."

Bohr's comments on other people's lectures were always meant to be encouraging and mild. His sardonic friend the nuclear physicist Paul Ehrenfest (1880–1933) used to urge him, "Just get on to the 'but,' and go from there."

One visiting lecturer to Bohr's institute was seen moping around the halls, sure that his talk had been a complete disaster. Why? "Well, Bohr said afterward that it had been very, very interesting."

THEN KLAUS FUCHS STARTED TAKING LOTS OF NOTES

During World War II, the physicists at Los Alamos developed a subculture all their own. Concern for security ran high, and everything related to the atom bomb had some kind of code name. "Uranium," for instance, was always spoken of as "tube alloy." When security was lifted after the war, Los Alamos veterans would blush when they heard the word "uranium" as if someone had said a dirty word.

Niels Bohr was at Los Alamos, but for security reasons everyone was supposed to call him "Nicholas Baker." This created problems for one young physicist giving a seminar. "Consider for simplicity," he said, "that a nucleus has a structure like that of the familiar Bohr atom." Hearing the forbidden word, his listeners smiled and looked at the floor. The young physicist stammered with confusion: "No, no—I mean, of course, a structure analogous to that of the familiar Baker atom!"

PROBABLY NOT EVEN A BAKER ATOM OF TRUTH IN THIS STORY

A scientist visiting the office of Niels Bohrs noticed a horseshoe nailed up over the door. "What is that for?" he asked.

"For good luck," replied Bohr.

"Surely you don't believe in that!" said the visitor.

"Of course not," said Bohr with a twinkle in his eye, "but they say it works whether you believe in it or not."

CELEBRATING THE WRONG DISCOVERY TWO HUNDRED YEARS EARLY

All too often, early scientists were unappreciated until after their deaths. One happy, if paradoxical, exception is the Hamburg alchemist Hennig Brand, the first person in recorded history to discover a chemical element. In 1669, after repeatedly distilling vats of his own urine, he obtained a remarkable white powder that glowed in the dark, or burned quickly giving off asphyxiating fumes.

Not only did Brand achieve the unprecedented feat of isolating a single element—phosphorus—but he also went proudly around Europe boasting that he had isolated a single element. How, you may wonder, did he know this? Mendeleyev's great periodic table lay two hundred years in the future, and Brand's contemporaries still thought of the universe as made up of earth, air, fire, and water.

Simple. Brand declared his magic powder was elemental fire.

WHAT AN INTERESTING STONE—NO, I DON'T WANT TO HOLD IT

A jeweler led the geologist William Buckland (1784–1856) to an important scientific discovery of an enormous deposit of coprolites. Buckland first noticed them being worn by fashionable London ladies in rings and brooches. (Coprolites, for those who don't know, are fossilized feces.)

COURANT EVENTS

Richard Courant (1888–1972), founder of the N.Y.U. mathematical institute that bears his name, came to the United States in 1934. Officially here on leave from his professorship in Göttingen, Courant was soon forced to "retire" from that post by Hitler's racial policies. On the official day set by the Nazis, the forty-six-year-old Courant wrote sadly to his friend James Franck, "Today I celebrated my sixty-eighth birthday."

The sheer scale of life in New York seemed daunting at first, but soon he and his wife, Nina, had formed a new circle of friends and fellow amateur musicians. One day an old acquaintance arrived for tea and asked, "Will you be playing quartets again in this country?" Courant smiled. "In this country, not quartets," he said. "In this country, octets."

THERE'LL ALWAYS BE AN ENGLAND

Charles Darwin's long voyage on board the *Beagle* opened his eyes to many things, but not to the glories of lands other than England.

As he explained in a letter to his sister Caroline, "I am determined and feel sure that the scenery of England is ten times more beautiful than any we have seen. What reasonable person can wish for great ill proportioned mountains, two and three miles high? No, no; give me the Brythen or some such compact little hill.—And then, as for your boundless plains and impenetrable forests, who would compare them with the green fields & oak woods of England?—People are pleased to talk of the ever smiling sky of the Tropics: must not this be precious nonsense? Who admires a lady's face who is always smiling? England is not one of your insipid beauties; she can cry, & frown, & smile, all by turns.—In short, I am convinced it is a most ridiculous thing to go round the world, when by staying quietly, the world will go round with you."

Darwin's preference for all things English extended even to its climate. To Darwin, on his way home at last, everything about his native land seemed utterly perfect. "How glad I shall be," he wrote, "when I can say like that good old Quarter Master who, entering the Channel on a gloomy November morning, exclaimed 'Ah, here there are none of those d————d blue skies.' "

NOT UNDER THE D————D BLUE SKIES, WE DO KNOW THAT

Although his theory of evolution made him famous, Darwin spent many years deeply involved in anatomical research. After seven years of studying the anatomy of barnacles, which he arranged to have sent to him from all over the world, Darwin complained, "I hate a barnacle as no man ever did before, not even a sailor in a slow-sailing ship."

To his children, of course, their father's preoccupations seemed entirely normal. One of Darwin's sons was taken out to tea at the home of some neighbors. After being shown all over their house and grounds by the family's children, he asked, "Yes, but where does your father do his barnacles?"

ELECTRICAL SHOCKER OF ALL TIME

Not many people realize that Nobel laureate Paul Adrien Maurice Dirac (1902–1984), the quintessential type of mathematical physicist, got his degree in electrical engineering! Dirac brought such precision and economy to everyday life that talking with him could be disconcerting. For instance, one evening his dinner partner idly remarked, "Isn't it windy today?"

No reply. Instead, Dirac excused himself, went to the door, looked out, then returned and sat down again.

"Yes," he said.

When Dirac was visiting the United States in 1929, a young college reporter for the *Wisconsin State News* decided to interview him. The conversation went something like this.

"Professor Dirac, is what you study difficult to understand?"

"Yes."

"Would you explain it for our readers?"

"No."

Long pause. The interviewer decided to shift to the human side of his subject. "Tell me, Professor Dirac, do you ever go to the movies?"

"Yes."

"When do you go to the movies?"

"In 1920. Perhaps also in 1930."

Dirac's minimalist elegance was not at all to the taste of Einstein's collaborator Paul Ehrenfest. According to Ehrenfest, "Elegance one should leave to tailors. (Die Eleganz soll man den Schneidern überlassen.)"

THE ONLY MAN TO CALL DIRAC A BIRDBRAIN

Young Dirac arrived at Niels Bohr's institute with a glowing recommendation from the great experimentalist Ernest Rutherford. A few months later, Bohr remarked to Rutherford that this marvelous Dirac hardly seemed so special: he said nothing and he did nothing. Legend has it that Rutherford replied with the following story:

A man went to a pet shop to buy a parrot. There was a gray parrot that knew a few words selling for one hundred dollars. There was a blue parrot that could sing and tell stories for two hundred dollars. There was a beautiful green and purple bird that spoke several ancient languages for five hundred dollars. And there was a nondescript brown bird priced at a thousand dollars.

"A thousand dollars!" exclaimed the would-be buyer. "That must be some bird—how many languages does he speak?"

"Just English," admitted the shopkeeper.

"His vocabulary is extraordinary, perhaps?"

The shopkeeper shrugged. "Not really."

"Does he sing, then?"

"No," said the shopkeeper. "Most days this parrot doesn't even talk."

"Well, does he do acrobatic tricks or something? What on earth is so valuable about that parrot?"

"Sir, this parrot *thinks*."

Rutherford concluded, "Dirac thinks."

PROVING THAT AT LEAST ONE OF HIS IDEAS WAS GOOD

Harry Ballot Clothiers on Princeton's Nassau Street is a haven for academics, a tradition dating back at least to the days of Albert Einstein. It seems that the great man refused to let his faithful assistant, Helen Dukas, throw out his very shabby raincoat. Certainly not! he told her. Why, a little trip to the dry-cleaners was all it needed.

Next day, Miss Dukas arrived at Harry Ballot's with the frayed coat over one arm. Could Mr. Wendroff please find her one exactly like it, only new? Between them, they removed the tags from the new coat, and packed it into a dry-cleaners bag.

Einstein's reaction? "You see, I told you dry-cleaning would make this coat as good as new."

WALK AND CHEW GUM, YES. WALK, CHEW GUM, AND SOLVE THE UNIFIED FIELD PROBLEM, NO.

Einstein walking the streets of Princeton lost in thought was a familiar sight during the thirties and forties. When his train of thought came to an end, he would go up to the nearest house, ring the bell, and explain, "I'm lost. Can you tell me how to get back to Mercer Street?"

Other times, when his thoughts became too heavy to carry around with him, he would just plunk himself down on a curbstone and close his eyes while untold equations paraded behind his eyelids. "But why is he doing that?" one little girl asked her mathematician father.

"Sssh," he whispered. "He sits on the concrete to think about the abstract!"

OH, YOU MEAN *THAT* INVITATION TO DINNER WITH THE PRESIDENT

During his years at the Institute for Advanced Study, Einstein often clashed with its high-handed first director, educational theorist Abraham Flexner. Flexner was strongly opposed to "his" faculty getting involved in politics, so much so that he once intercepted and refused a dinner invitation sent to Einstein by President Roosevelt. Einstein only learned of the invitation by chance, during a conversation several months later with Felix Frankfurter. Ah well, Flexner blandly explained when confronted, he had thought it too trivial a matter to mention.

SO MAYBE FLEXNER WAS GLAD WHEN LATER THINGS HEATED UP

The conflicts between Flexner and Einstein were prefigured at one of their earliest meetings, in 1931, at Einstein's summer home in Potsdam. The day was cold and rainy. As the two men shook hands, Flexner, who was shivering despite a heavy raincoat worn over his warm wool suit, looked curiously at his host, completely at ease in a lightweight suit of summer flannels. "Are you really warm enough?" asked Flexner through chattering teeth.

"Yes," replied Einstein. "Besides, I dress according to the season, not the weather. This is summer."

AND IF YOU TURN ON A LIGHT, IT'S GUARANTEED TO MOVE FASTER THAN YOUR TOE

Einstein showed up at the Institute one morning hobbling around with a cane. It seems that during the night he had stubbed his big toe. "This has happened five or six times before from walking around in the darkness," he explained to Flexner. "The only really annoying part of it is that every time I have to have an x-ray taken to be sure no bones are broken."

Flexner asked if it wouldn't save trouble to turn on a light.

"Oh," said Einstein, "I never thought of that."

BUT THEN AGAIN, NEITHER IS THE NAVY

One of Einstein's former secretaries was applying for a military job in wartime, so Einstein submitted to being grilled about her suitability by an earnest young Navy lieutenant. How long had Einstein known this woman? Did she have a good reputation in the community? Was she a loyal citizen?

Einstein was a little puzzled by this line of questioning. "What kind of a job is Miss X applying for?" he asked.

"Naval Intelligence," replied the officer.

Einstein shook his head. "You *certainly* cannot hire Miss X for Naval Intelligence."

"Why not?" the officer eagerly demanded.

"Because," Einstein said, "Miss X is not intelligent."

A MODEL ANSWER YIELDS SOME RELATIVE TRANQUILITY

Einstein in America found himself engulfed by fame. Autograph seekers pursued him everywhere. Society matrons ran their fingers through his hair. A chance remark he made during a walk—"Raffiniert ist der Herr Gott, aber boshaft ist er nicht" (God is subtle but not malicious)—wound up engraved in marble over a fireplace at the Princeton math department. He had to abandon his magnificent ground-floor office there because sightseers kept peering through his window.

A quiet, scholarly man, Einstein was sometimes overwhelmed by this relentless public attention. And all the while, his face grew more and more famous because of the many patient hours he spent posing for refugee artists who needed the money they could make by creating yet another Einstein portrait.

One day, Einstein was riding the train from New York to Princeton, when his reverie was interrupted by an inquisitive stranger who said, "I don't think I know you—but your face is so familiar . . . How could that be?"

Einstein said wearily, "Perhaps because I spend my days as an artists' model."

"Ah," said the man, "*that's* why I know your face!" And he left Einstein in peace for the rest of the trip.

THERE MIGHT HAVE BEEN OTHER COMPLEX VARIABLES INVOLVED

There were those among Einstein's colleagues who got tired of his celebrity, and even a few who suspected that his trademark disheveled dress and wild mane of extra-long hair were not entirely accidental. After all, as Otto Neugebauer pointed out, if you are absent-minded and neglect your hair, does it stand out all over your head? No! It gets tangled and lies down flat. To have hair sticking out like Einstein's takes work!

One day at tea in Princeton's old Fine Hall, Einstein was lamenting the number of autograph hunters who pestered him as he tried to walk across the campus. "I would do anything to get rid of those people, anything!" he lamented.

"I can tell you how to get rid of them," said Salomon Bochner brusquely.

"Oh, if you would only tell me, I should be so grateful! I would do anything for anonymity!"

"In that case," said Bochner, "get a decent haircut."

GOSH, MR. NAPOLEON, LOST AGAIN?

Einstein was very fond of children, and the Princeton children loved him in return. "I talked to Einstein today," a little girl reported to her mother.

"What did you say?"

"He said, 'Hello, little girl,' and I said, 'Hello, Einstein!' "

"My dear," gasped her mother, "you should have addressed him as 'Professor Einstein.' "

The little girl was unrepentant. "But that would be silly, Mummy. You wouldn't call Napoleon 'Mr. Napoleon,' would you?"

AND HE WOULDN'T CALL HIM "MR. EINSTEIN" EITHER

Einstein's long hair looked especially strange in an era when acceptable styles for men and women were sharply differentiated. One little boy expressed this apparent contradiction by asking plaintively, "But why doesn't *he* cut *her* hair?"

DESPITE RELIGIOUSLY TRYING TO STAY OUT OF TROUBLE

In 1913 the drivers of horse trams in Oxford were striking for higher wages. Police kept the striking drivers from stopping the black-legs brought in to replace them—until the biologist J. B. S. Haldane (1892–1964), then a student at Oxford, intervened.

His method was unorthodox but effective. "I walked up and down Cornmarket Street chanting the Athanasian Creed and the hymeneal psalm *Eructavit cor meum* in a loud but unmelodious voice. A large crowd collected. The police ineffectively pushed pious old ladies into the gutter. The trams failed to penetrate the crowd, and their horses were detached and wandered off in an aimless manner. The strike was successful and as the trams could no longer yield a profit, they were replaced by motor omnibuses, which were capable both of higher speed and higher wages."

As for Haldane, the authorities fined him two guineas, "the first case for over three centuries when a man was punished in Oxford for publicly professing the principles of the Church of England."

MOST LECTURERS PREFER A BOHR-ING ASSESSMENT

Both Niels Bohr and his mathematician brother, Harald, spent time in Göttingen, but it was not there Bohr learned to deal gently with mediocre speakers. David Hilbert (1862–1943) ran the Göttingen Mathematics Club with a hand of purest Prussian iron. "Only the raisins in the cake" was his rule for speakers, and if a lecturer began to describe his computations Hilbert would brusquely interrupt with, "We are not here to check that the sign is right."

Hilbert could be brutal on occasion. Once he interrupted a speaker in midlecture to announce, "My dear colleague, I am very much afraid that you do not know what a differential equation is." The humiliated speaker fled to the next room, which happened to be a reading room. Some others in the audience reproached Hilbert, but he persisted, "He *doesn't* know what a differential equation is. Now, you see, he has gone to the reading room to look it up."

FERTILE IF UNMENTIONABLE DISCOVERY

Alexander von Humboldt (1769–1859) spent the years from 1799 to 1804 traveling throughout South America. His mapping of Earth's magnetic field later provided important confirmation to the theory of continental drift. Humboldt learned much by talking with Indians along the Amazon about their own observations and theories. On the other hand, a great shower of meteors was explained by the natives as "urine from the stars."

Humboldt discovered among many other things the enormous mounds of South American guano that were to increase European food production during the nineteenth century. He was probably just as happy his name was given, not to those reeking deposits left by generations of seabirds, but to the cold-water current off the coast of Peru.

UNMENTIONABLE BUT NOT, ALAS, UNMENTIONED

Alexander von Humboldt's discoveries made him one of the most famous men in Europe, to his great annoyance. Often he would try to retreat to his study, pleading with his old Swiss servant to keep all visitors away. It was the honest servant's practice to greet Humboldt's callers with the information, "My master is in, but he wants me to say that he's not."

IT SEEMED LIKE A NATURAL SELECTION

Darwin's great contemporary T. H. Huxley (1825–1895), whose spirited defense of the theory of evolution won him the nickname of "Darwin's bulldog," came from a poor family. Only a special scholarship for "young Gentlemen of respectable but unfortunate families" enabled him to go to medical school. When his researches won him a gold medal from England's Royal Society, he ended up having to sell it to pay his brother's debts.

As loyal to his beliefs as to his unfortunate family, Huxley spent much of his later life taking on battles that Darwin preferred to avoid. One famous debate on evolution was staged in 1860 between Huxley and Samuel Wilberforce, the Bishop of Oxford. Wilberforce chose to dodge the scientific issues, instead poking fun at what he considered Darwin's absurdities. He concluded his speech by asking Huxley to tell the audience whether it was through his grandfather or his grandmother that he claimed to be descended from a monkey.

"The Lord hath delivered him into mine hands," muttered Huxley to his neighbor as he rose to reply to his sneering opponent.

"If the question is put to me," he said, "would I rather have a miserable ape for a grandfather, or a man highly endowed by nature and possessed of great means of influence, and yet who employs these faculties and influence for the mere purpose of introducing ridicule into a grave scientific discussion—I unhesitatingly affirm my preference for the ape."

AT LEAST WITH HUXLEY YOU DON'T GET LOTS OF BEETLES

To the end of his life, Huxley claimed to be baffled by the reaction of Victorian religious leaders. "After all," he pointed out, "it is as respectable to be modified monkey as to be modified dirt."

In 1882, Huxley happened to be visiting the United States at the time Johns Hopkins was just being opened, and Daniel Coit Gilman invited him to be the first speaker at the ceremony. Eager to stress the secular nature of his new institution, Gilman also gave orders that no invocation or prayers of any kind would be part of the proceedings.

Both acts were considered signs of shocking impiety. In the words of a local minister, " 'Twas an ill thing to have invited Professor Huxley. 'Twere better to have invited God. 'Twould have been absurd to ask them both."

NEVER MIND THE FELLOW'S GRANDPARENTS, LOOK AT HIS GRANDCHILDREN

T. H. Huxley's grandchildren included the novelist Aldous Huxley, the noted biologist Sir Julian Huxley, and 1963 Nobel laureate Andrew Fielding Huxley.

History records this early verdict of one very independent scientist on another (T. H. on Julian): "I like that chap. I like the way he looks you right in the eye and disobeys you."

GOOD REASON TO BE BLUE JEANS

Sir James Jeans (1877–1946) was the author of the Steady State theory of galaxy formation, a long-time rival of the Big Bang model. In 1951, while the issue was still hotly debated in scientific circles, the Big Bang became an unquestionable religious truth when Pope Pius XII publicly embraced it, telling the Pontifical Academy of Sciences that "from one to ten thousand million years ago, the matter of the (known) spiral nebulae was compressed into a relatively restricted space, at the time the cosmic processes had their beginning."

Jeans might have taken a gloomy view of the future of the human race had he been able to foresee that even in the midtwentieth century a respectable scientific theory would suffer the ecclesiastical fate of Galileo's.

IN WHICH CASE, DON'T SIGN ANY LONG LEASES

Sir James Jeans on the prospects immediately before us: "Taking a very gloomy view of the future of the human race, let us suppose that it can only expect to survive for two thousand million years longer."

SOON TO BE LESS BLUE JEANS

Sir James Jeans's mnemonic for the first fourteen decimal places of pi suggests, however, that the future may hold some cheering consolations:

"How I want a drink, alcoholic of course, after the heavy
3(.)1   4   1   5   9   2   6   5   3   5
chapters involving quantum mechanics."
8   9   7   9

DEGREES CABLE? WHAT WITH CENTIGRADE AND CELSIUS, WE HAVE TOO MANY DEGREES "C" ALREADY.

Young William Thomson (1824–1907), better known later as Lord Kelvin, began attending his father's mathematics lectures at Glasgow University when he was only eight. If a difficult question had stumped the other students, he would pipe up, "Please, papa, please do let me answer!"

He became a fully enrolled student there at the age of ten, and later attended Cambridge University. He was only twenty-two when Glasgow offered him its professorship of natural philosophy, a post he then held for fifty-three years despite many other offers.

When the British Association held its annual meeting in Edinburgh in 1871, he was, of course, asked to be its president. The result could have been disastrous, for he lost his ticket and the porter refused to admit him without one. "But this is Sir William Thomson, the President of the Association," urged a bystander.

The porter's stony reply: "I have orders aboot tickets. I have nae orders aboot Presidents."

In addition to his important work on thermodynamics, he played an important role in laying the first transatlantic cable and improving the compass used by mariners. When Queen Victoria made him a peer, in 1896, the titles "Lord Cable" and "Lord Compass" were both considered. Fortunately, the name of the River Kelvin, on whose banks Glasgow University stands, was finally chosen instead.

KELVIN'S CLASS ASSIGNMENT

One day, Lord Kelvin posted a notice on the door of the lecture hall: "Professor Thomson will not meet his classes today." Students erased the C and chortled over the result: "Professor Thomson will not meet his lasses today." When they arrived for his next lecture, they found he had altered the sign again, to express his opinion of their humor. It now read: "Professor Thomson will not meet his asses today."

LEFSCHETZ HIMSELF COULD SPEAK RIGHT TO THE POINT

Solomon Lefschetz (1884–1972), the mathematician who coined the English word "topology," was a remarkable figure in many ways. Trained as an engineer, he turned to mathematics in 1907 after an industrial accident cost him both his hands.

An inspired teacher and a brilliant researcher, Lefschetz still found plenty of time to feud with other mathematicians. His behavior at seminars inspired Princeton students to create the following verse:

> *Here's to Papa Solomon L.,*
> *Unpredictable as hell,*
> *When laid at last beneath the sod*
> *He'll start right in to heckle God.*

One favorite enemy was R. L. Moore. Lefschetz was an exponent of algebraic topology, and had little patience with the R. L. Moore school of point-set topology. According to Lefschetz, "To write a book about topology and confine yourself to Moore's subject matter is like writing a book about zoology and confining yourself to the rhinoceros."

Despite his bluntness, Lefschetz's open-hearted generosity made him widely beloved, at least by people he wasn't feuding with. When the Princeton mathematics department got a beautiful new building, they ordered an expensive pushbutton lock to provide security for Lefschetz's office. (His metal hands made it hard to use an ordinary key.) Delighted with this new toy, Lefschetz eagerly showed everyone he met exactly how to work the lock and get into his office.

Born in Moscow and raised in France, Lefschetz had a linguistic advantage at foreign conferences. Lawrence Markus quotes his instantaneous translation for some colleagues of a half-hour mathematical lecture delivered in rapid-fire Russian: "He says, 'you try to get the final formula from the first one.' "

LINNAEUS, PLANT PORNOGRAPHER?

Wilfred Blunt's biography of the great Swedish botanist Carl Linnaeus (1707–1778) is full of fascinating details about his life. For instance, Blunt quotes Linnaeus's own account of the time of his birth (May 23, 1707): "at one o'clock in the morning, between the month of growing and the month of flowering, when the cuckoo was announcing the imminence of summer, when the trees were in leaf but before the season of blossom."

Linnaeus made a long and fruitful journey to study the natural history of Lapland. Every aspect of Lapp life depends on a family's reindeer. Because a gelded reindeer is so far superior in size, tenderness, and docility to its normal counterpart, one of the most flattering ways to praise an eighteenth-century Lapp was to call him (or her) a real *uœrtzeketz*, meaning "castrated reindeer."

Linnaeus's notebooks and letters present a vivid picture of his contemporaries; for example, this account of the hard-drinking style of the miners of Falun: "The foundry owners put a firkin on the table, and the cups race over the table as briskly as the piss-pot under it."

Linnaeus's pioneering system for classifying plants was based on a careful study of the distinguishing characteristics to be found in their sexual organs. His straightforward accounts of plant reproduction were considered shocking by many. "Who would have thought that bluebells, lilies, and onions could be up to such harlotry?" asked one astounded reader. "A literal translation of the first principles of Linnaean botany is enough to shock female modesty," scolded the Reverend Samuel Goodenough. "It is possible that many virtuous students might not be able to make out the similitude of *Clitoria*."

Linnaeus was no free-thinker, but a respectable householder who went to Mass every Sunday with his dog Pompe by his side. Once the service had lasted an hour, however, Linnaeus got up and went home whether the sermon was finished or not. History records that even when Linnaeus was sick, Pompe went to the usual service, and, after the customary hour, got up and went home to his master.

MORDELL DEMONSTRATES A SIDESTEP

The story goes that the great mathematician L. J. Mordell (1888–1972) was making a postwar lecture tour of the United States. One evening, the phone rang in his motel room. "Good evening!" said the caller, with enthusiasm and a strong midwestern accent. "Can you by any chance tell me the name of the first president of the United States?"

"George Washington," said Mordell.

"Congratulations!" said his caller. "You have just won ten free dance lessons from the Eleganté Dance Studios of downtown Kansas City."

"I see," said Mordell slowly. "But perhaps you could also give me some information. Who was president of the United States during the Civil War?"

"Abraham Lincoln?" said the caller.

"Congratulations to you!" said Mordell. "Why, you have just won those ten free dance lessons back."

AND FOR READERSHIP HE DIDN'T GIVE A FIG

Sir Isaac Newton (1642–1726), born in Lincolnshire on Christmas day, claimed his first scientific experiment was made when he was fifteen, on the day of Cromwell's death. On that day a great storm swept over England. Newton measured its strength by jumping both with and against the wind to compare how far he could leap in either direction.

Like many scientists, Newton was noted for his absentmindedness. When he left home for Cambridge, the family servants rejoiced at the departure of one who was good for nothing but to go to university. During his student years, he so often forgot the meals brought to his room that his cat grew fat from eating them. As a don, Newton rarely came to the common table. When he did, he was as likely as not to be so absorbed in thought that he forgot to eat before his dishes were carried away.

Supposedly, when Newton was once asked how he discovered the law of universal gravitation, he replied, "By thinking on it continuously."

In 1771, Newton's friend William Stukeley arrived at the annual Lincolnshire Feast in London to find Newton quietly seated downstairs while all the principal men of the county were upstairs. When the local dignitaries heard that Newton was there, they urged Stukeley to invite him upstairs to the "chief room." "The chief room is the room where Sir Isaac Newton is," retorted Stukeley. So the upper room was left deserted as everyone flocked downstairs to join Sir Isaac.

Newton's *Principia* is probably one of the few scientific works made difficult to read on purpose. Newton explained that he hoped to avoid many pointless arguments if only those very well grounded in mathematics could read his book.

DON'T LOOK NOW, BUT THERE HAS BEEN AN EQUAL AND OPPOSITE REACTION

Newton pointed out that Earth's rotation would give it a pumpkin shape, bulging at the equator. In the 1730s, two French expeditions fought off wolves and other obstacles to make careful measurements that confirmed his prediction. The French mathematician Maupertuis, who had been among those dispatched to Lapland, received the following note from his friend Voltaire:

> *Vous avez confirmé dans les lieux pleins d'ennui*
> *Ce que Newton connût sans sortir de chez lui.*

(Roughly, "It took you an arduous journey to confirm what Newton understood without leaving home.")

Newton's triumph was so complete that soon Voltaire began to complain about the overwhelming popularity of science. "Fine literature is hardly any longer the fashion in Paris. Everyone works at geometry and physics. Everyone has a hand at argument. Sentiment, imagination, and the finer arts are banished. Not that I am angry that science is being cultivated, but I don't want it to become a tyrant that excludes all else."

> *Nature and Nature's laws lay hid in night.*
> *God said, "Let Newton be!" and all was light.*
> ALEXANDER POPE
> *It did not last: the Devil howling "Ho,*
> *Let Einstein be," restored the status quo.*
> J. C. SQUIRE

AND WHAT A BOMB IT WOULD HAVE BEEN WITHOUT HIM

Scientists who did not go to Harvard can take comfort from the life of Linus Pauling (1901–), two-time Nobel Prize winner, whose undergraduate alma mater is Oregon Agricultural College. An early scientific discovery dating from this period came when Pauling and a friend serenaded a girls' dormitory one dark night. "I just confirmed a scientific fact here," Pauling reported in a whisper. "The angle of incidence is greater than the angle of reflection, so I can piss against this tree without making any noise!"

Pauling's work on the structure of protein, using x-ray crystallography techniques developed by W. L. Bragg, won him worldwide eminence. At home, his political views made him suspect (this was the McCarthy era), and for years Pauling could attend no international conferences because the State Department refused to give him a passport. Finally, and after many delays, they consented to issue one in 1954—barely in time for him to receive that year's Nobel Prize for chemistry.

LIFE AND NONDEATH OF BERTRAND RUSSELL

The mathematician Bertrand Russell (1872–1970) was eleven when his brother Frank introduced to him the joys of Euclid. Bertrand, who was later to be accused of spending three hundred pages to show that "one plus one equals two," enjoyed Euclid's definitions but balked at the idea that axioms had to be accepted without proof. He only consented to them when Frank refused to go on unless he did.

Mathematics later stood him in good stead when, as a young man, he was haunted by thoughts of death. As a Cambridge student, Russell wrote, "I did not, however, commit suicide because I wished to know more of mathematics." On another gloomy occasion, he dreamed he was visited in his bedroom by Benjamin Jowett, the famous Master of Balliol at Oxford. "Don't do it, young man," said this ghostly vision. "Don't do it: you will live to regret it."

Russell probably lived to regret many things over the near-century spanned by his life, but suicide was not one of them. Thanks to Euclid and Jowett, the baby whose free-thinking parents provided him with the great Victorian thinker John Stuart Mill as a godfather (nonreligious, of course) grew up to lecture President Kennedy on his conduct of the Cuban missile crisis.

A REMARKABLE TRANSFORMATION

Ernest Rutherford (1871–1937) discovered the atomic nucleus because he needed to come up with a quick project for one of his many students. Hans Geiger, inventor of the radiation counter that bears his name, pointed out to Rutherford that it was about time for Ernest Marsden (later Sir Ernest) to try some work on his own. Rutherford had been observing the deflection of alpha-particles by the atoms in a thin sheet of gold foil, so he idly remarked that "young Marsden" might as well see if any bounced back at very sharp angles.

Since at that time no one conceived of the atom as mostly empty space with a tiny massive nucleus, Marsden was expected to see nothing at all. His positive result amazed Rutherford as much as anyone. "It was as though you had fired a fifteen-inch shell at a piece of tissue paper and it had bounced back and hit you," he later remarked.

Rutherford considered himself a physicist, and when his work on radioactive transmutation of elements earned him the 1908 Nobel Prize in chemistry, he liked to joke that the Swedish Academy had decided to subject *him* to "instantaneous transmutation."

TALK ABOUT LAST RESORTS!

Someone once charged that it was a little too easy for Rutherford to make great discoveries—he was always riding the crest of a wave. "Well, I made the wave, didn't I?" retorted Rutherford.

His deceptively modest explanation for the preeminence of British science is also worth recording: "We haven't much money so we've got to use our brains."

MEETING RESISTANCE, HE WENT OHM

Charles Proteus Steinmetz (1865–1923), an electrical engineer whose genius lived up to his middle name, worked at General Electric for many years. One morning he arrived at his office to find there had been a change in policy overnight. On his desk, someone had posted a tidy cardboard sign saying "No Smoking." Steinmetz took out his pen, relettered the sign so that now it read "No Smoking—No Steinmetz," and departed. The policy was changed.

CIRCUITOUS REASONING

One day a whole roomful of General Electric's most expensive machinery went out of order. By this time Steinmetz had retired, but the company's baffled engineers called him back as a consultant. Steinmetz ambled from machine to machine, taking a measurement here, scribbling something in his notebook there. After about an hour, he took out a piece of chalk and marked a large 'X' on the casing of one machine. Workers pried off the casing and found the problem at once. But when company executives got Steinmetz's bill for $10,000, they were reluctant to pay it. "This seems a bit excessive for one chalk mark," Steinmetz was told. "Perhaps you'd better itemize your charges."

Within a few days, they received the following itemized bill from Steinmetz:

Making one chalk mark:	$1.00
Knowing where to make one chalk mark:	$9,999.00

I THINK HE'S THE FELLOW WHO MARRIED A PAGET

J. J. Thomson (1856–1940), the son of a Manchester bookseller, rose to become Sir Joseph John Thomson, head of the Cavendish Laboratory and winner of the 1906 Nobel Prize in physics for his discovery of the electron. Among his old neighbors was a boy who left school early but grew up to be a substantial manufacturer.

Many years later, a banquet was given in the manufacturer's honor, where he denounced the futility of education, using his own case as an illustration. "When I was a boy in school," he said, "the teachers were always praising a student named Johnny Thomson. The rest of us were constantly told to try to be more like little Johnny Thomson. Well, who ever hears of little Johnny Thomson *now*?"

In his old age, J. J. Thomson remained a handsome man, with long white hair at a time when it was not fashionable to have long hair, very gentle, and much beloved by his grandchildren. His wife, on the other hand, was an intimidating presence. In contrast to Thomson's modest origins, her lineage was distinguished and very long. No one who knew her was likely to forget for long that Mrs. Thomson was, in fact, a Paget.

Someone once complimented her on the intelligence of her grand-children (the children of G. W. Thomson, yet another family Nobel Prize winner). The old lady accepted the praise with a sigh. "Yes," she said, "but if only they had the *Paget* brains!"

BRITISH RETICENCE IMPEDES A SEARCH FOR NAKED TRUTH

Sir Joseph John Thomson, the discoverer of the electron, grew rather absent-minded in his old age. One day, when he had not reappeared from his usual afternoon nap, his wife went upstairs to wake him. He was gone.

Then, to her dismay, she noticed that all the clothes he had been wearing that morning were also gone—with the exception of his trousers, still draped across the back of a chair. Imagining the scandal throughout Cambridge should the Master of Trinity be wandering somewhere with no trousers, she quickly telephoned the college gate-keeper's lodge.

"Have you seen the Master this afternoon?"

"Yes, your ladyship."

"Did the Master go out of the gate when you saw him?"

"Yes, your ladyship."

Of course, one cannot bluntly ask if he was wearing his trousers! "And did he—did he look well?"

(Actually, Thomson turned up later that afternoon in an old pair of gardening trousers, so scandal was averted.)

MATHEMATICAL JOHNNY ON THE SPOT

John von Neumann (1907–1957) combined a photographic memory with breathtaking mathematical power. He could quote page after page of a novel read twenty years before, or invent on the spur of a moment a proof of someone else's brand-new result. "Most mathematicians prove what they can, von Neumann proves what he wants," went one popular saying during his heyday. But von Neumann was no mere prover of other people's theorems—he played a seminal role in the creation of many diverse fields, among them game theory and computers.

In Budapest, von Neumann had been a child prodigy, and he always claimed that after a certain age a mathematician's powers start to wane. That age was gradually raised as von Neumann himself got older—though in an effort at modesty, he always set it a few years younger than his current age.

Modesty did not come naturally to von Neumann, and it is hard to see why it would. Once, after a very rare failure to finish a proof he had begun during a lecture, von Neumann lamented, "I knew three different ways of proving this result, but unfortunately I chose a fourth."

On another occasion, someone asked him, "What percentage of mathematics might a person aspire to understand today?" After a brief thinking trance, von Neumann replied decisively, "About 28 percent."

---

and the answer is:
GAME, SET, AND MATCH.

and the question is:
Name two theories invented by von Neumann,
and an incendiary device.

TEACHING SCIENCE

CLEAR-SIGHTED WITH OR WITHOUT HIS MICROSCOPE

Antonie van Leeuwenhoek (1632–1723), the Dutch dry-goods salesman who introduced the world of science to his microscope, refused to spend time teaching others his methods. "I've never taught one, because if I taught one, I'd have to teach others," he explained to Leibniz. "I would give myself over to slavery, whereas I want to stay a free man.

"The professors and students of the University of Leyden were long ago so dazzled by my discoveries, they hired three lens grinders to come to teach the students, but what came of it? Nothing, so far as I can judge, for almost all of the courses they teach there are for the purpose of getting money through knowledge or for gaining the respect of the world by showing people how learned you are, and these have nothing to do with discovering the things that are buried from our eyes."

Scientists Who Can't Teach, Teach Anyway

ONE MAY BE REAL, BUT IT ISN'T REALLY VARIABLE

Sometimes people get stuck giving courses outside their own specialty—sometimes it works out, and sometimes it doesn't. The logician Alonzo Church (1903–) was once assigned to teach a course in real variables. Around Christmas, however, the chairman miraculously found another volunteer to teach the course. This may also have something to do with the fact that Church had been so careful in laying the logical foundations for real variables that the first three months had gotten his lectures only as far as the number one.

AN OBVIOUS SLANDER OF GREAT MATHEMATICIANS

Mathematicians use the word *obvious* to mean . . . just about what they want it to mean. Someone once translated the term for Princeton audiences as follows: If Alonzo Church says something is obvious, the students saw it half an hour ago. If Hermann Weyl says it's obvious, von Neumann *might* be able to prove it. If Solomon Lefschetz says it's obvious, it's probably wrong.

BUT THIS IS SAID TO BE A TRUE STORY ABOUT WIENER

At M.I.T., also, the term *obvious* comes in for abuse as well as use. "And the result follows here quite obviously," the cyberneticist Norbert Wiener (1894–1964) once told a class.

One student timidly raised his hand and said, "Professor Wiener, I'm afraid I don't see it."

"Very well," said Wiener, "Perhaps I can derive it by some other method." He gazed into space for a moment, then nodded. "Yes," he said, "by a completely different method precisely the same result." He beamed at the student.

"But, Professor Wiener, I still don't understand."

Wiener looked stern. "Young man, if you can't understand such a simple matter as this, having seen it derived by two quite different methods, I am afraid you will never be a mathematician!"

AS SIMPLE AS ABC? WELL, NOT QUITE

The typical Lefschetz lecture has been described as follows: He says A, he writes B, he means C, the students think he said D, and he goes home believing he's also covered E.

This story has also attached itself to other beloved but confusing lecturers.

SPEAKING OF OTHER LECTURERS . . .

J. H. C. Whitehead (1904–1960) built an important school of topology at Oxford, in spite of student claims that those initials stood not for "John Henry Constantine," but for "Jesus, He's Confusing!"

Tired of forever being asked about the philosophical work of his uncle, Alfred North Whitehead, J. H. C. finally worked up a stock reply: "I don't really think about it much. Tell me, what do you think of *your* uncle's philosophy?"

A MATHEMATICIAN'S DRINKING PROBLEM

The new calculus professor is about to begin her course of lectures. Next to the podium she places her notes and two large glasses, one of them full of water. A student asks, "What is the empty glass for?"

"Isn't it obvious?" the professor says. "That's in case I *don't* get thirsty."

BUT WHAT WOULD BE THE POINT OF SAYING SO?

The topologist R. L. Moore was famous for—among other things—his unorthodox teaching style. Moore believed that students should *not* be taught. He prepared for a course by removing all books on the subject from the University of Texas library, forcing his students to derive every theorem and prove every result with no assistance. In class, he did not lecture—he asked questions. To this day, it is said, the Socratic method is always referred to in Texas as "the R. L. Moore method." Surviving his courses was very much sink-or-swim, but they produced a whole generation of top-notch American mathematicians.

With the top-notch mathematicians of his own generation, R. L. Moore indulged in many bitter feuds. When Moore was selected to give the AMS Colloquium Lectures in 1932, everyone expected sparks to fly in Princeton, the home turf of his archrival, Solomon Lefschetz.

"Let A be a point," Moore began his first lecture, "and let B be a point."

Lefschetz leaped to his feet. "Why not just say, 'Let A and B be points'?" he demanded.

"Because," said Moore triumphantly, "they might both be the same point!"

MOORE MIGHT HAVE GRASPED THE POINT OF THIS, I THINK

"Let us suppose," began the professor, "that x is the shortest distance between these two points."

A student protested. "But, then suppose in the end x turns out *not* to be the shortest distance between those two points?"

SOCRATES MEETS THE WILD (MID)WEST

R. L. Moore may have been born to be a Texan, but this incident dates from his early career at Northwestern. The math department chairman heard that Moore was going around campus with a pistol. When he approached Moore about this, he found him eager to explain.

The problem was that in one course there were some students Moore suspected of making fun of him when his back was turned. He hadn't caught them yet, but when he did he planned to whirl around and shoot in their direction. "But you have nothing to worry about," Moore assured the chairman. "I won't miss them by much, but I'll miss them. I'm a very good shot."

THE WILD, WILD WEST OF DENMARK

Niels Bohr enjoyed an occasional cowboy movie, but complained they were all too unbelievable. "That the scoundrel runs off with the beautiful girl is logical, it always happens. That the bridge collapses under their carriage is unlikely but I am willing to accept it. That the heroine remains suspended in midair over a precipice is even more unlikely, but again I accept it. I am even willing to accept that at that very moment Tom Mix is coming by on his horse. But at that very moment there should be a fellow with a motion picture camera to film the whole business, that is more than I am willing to believe."

Bohr's interest in cowboys led him to speculate on the scientific theory of gunfighting. Bohr argued that the first to reach for his gun will actually lose, because an action resulting from conscious decision is slower than one made as a reflex response. Some students disagreed, and several of them bought toy pistols to try it out with Bohr. In duel after duel, he was always able to fire first.

MORE = OR = LESS MATHEMATICAL COWBOYS

A new deputy was being briefed by the old sheriff. "Now, son, suppose you see an outlaw running out of the bank, his gun at the ready. What do you do?"

"Pull out my six-gun and shoot him," said the eager deputy.

"Well, but now suppose you see *two* outlaws running out of the bank, their guns at the ready, what do you do?"

"Pull out my six-gun and shoot them both," came the prompt reply.

"Well, but now suppose you see *ten* outlaws running out of the bank, their guns at the ready. What are you going to do?"

"Pull out my six-gun and shoot them all," said the deputy.

"But, son, think about it—where are you going to get all them bullets?"

"Why, the same place you're getting all them outlaws, I reckon."

TOUGH TALKING FROM THE LECTURER'S POINT OF VIEW

Rutherford was a genius in the laboratory—and also in the lecture hall! As a very young man, he once found himself trying to demonstrate some apparatus that would not cooperate. After several futile attempts, Rutherford calmly told his distinguished audience, "Something has gone wrong. If you would all like to go for a stroll and a smoke for five minutes it will be working on your return." It was.

"That young man will go a long way," remarked one farsighted member of his audience.

In 1904 Rutherford addressed the Royal Institution of London. He later described his experience as follows:

I came into the room, which was half dark, and presently spotted Lord Kelvin in the audience and realised that I was in for trouble at the last part of my speech dealing with the age of the Earth, where my views conflicted with his. To my relief Kelvin fell fast asleep, but as I came to the important point, I saw the old bird sit up, open an eye, and cock a baleful glance at me. Then a sudden inspiration came and I said Lord Kelvin had limited the age of the Earth, provided no new source was discovered. That prophetic utterance referred to what we are now considering tonight, radium! Behold! the old boy beamed upon me.

NOTES ON A LECTURE

If I could solve equations that I write,
I would not be here lecturing tonight,
Because you'd see how trivial it is
To understand my model. But, gee whiz!
It's easier to let computers run
Than think, or labor underneath the sun
To see how nature actually acts.
(And please do not confuse me with the facts.)

I beg you, treat with greatest tenderness
The tables, numbers, formulas and graphs
That I here tentatively lay before
You, barely able clearly to express
What tremulous excitement in me laughs!
Could understanding truth delight me more?

                                          J.E.C.

MORE OR LESS THE OPPOSITE OF SIMPLE INTEREST

Peter Winkler, a mathematician at Bell Communications Research, was delivering a lecture at Rutgers. "Now this case is not very interesting," he said, then paused. "But the reason *why* it's not interesting is really interesting, so let me tell you about it."

AND IT'S A TYPE GEE-WHIZ STAR

The distinguished astrophysicist had been invited to address a large group of amateur stargazers. Unfortunately, he chose to address his sophisticated New York audience at about a fifth-grade level. The last straw, for one listener at least, came when the speaker told them reassuringly: "Now, the structure of the sun is *very* simple."

Came a voice from the audience: "From a parsec away, you look pretty simple yourself!"

YOU WOULD HAVE PREFERRED A SINGALONG OF "FLY ME TO THE MOON"?

Another astronomy professor was coaxed into addressing a group of alumni on planetary exploration. He did his best, but the audience was restless. At the reception following his talk, one tipsy old-boy cornered him and said, "Y'know, I just spent an hour listening to you, and I don't think it left me one bit the wiser."

"No doubt you are right," said the professor courteously. "But you are now somewhat better informed."

---

and the question is:
What's white when it's dirty and black when it's clean?

and the answer is:
A blackboard.

TWO-FISTED TEACHING METHODS

My freshman chem prof had a trick that kept us fascinated every time he went to the blackboard. With the chalk in his left hand, he would start scribbling down some long chemical formula; then midway through it the chalk would switch to his right hand and he'd keep on going just as fast as ever.

The mathematician Felix Klein is said to have gone one better by doing the same stunt with a cigar in the nonwriting hand. Students took bets that someday Klein would stick the chalk in his mouth or write with the cigar, but no one ever collected on it.

Anyway, the Harvard professor in this supposedly true story was probably their spiritual cousin. He was famous for being able to fill up the four sliding blackboards in his class in about the first fifteen minutes. One day, as he finished the first board and slid it up, he found chalked on the board underneath,

PLEASE SLOW DOWN.

Not only that, but the next board he slid up revealed,

THANKS.

BUT—PLEASE SLOW DOWN

A LITTLE MORE?

YOUR MOTHER TOLD YOU YOU SHOULD GO TO HARVARD

Then there was the Caltech student with the opposite complaint. One of his professors had written a book on the subject he was teaching, and each lecture reproduced a chapter at slow and careful length. An hour of this was more than flesh could stand. So the student rigged up the lecture hall clock to run faster. In that classroom, an hour lasted only fifty minutes—after a week it was reduced to forty-five—another week more, and the student adjusted it to forty. He had the poor professor racing through his chapter in half an hour by the time they finally caught him.

WHERE IS THAT CALTECH STUDENT WHEN YOU NEED HIM?

"I'm sorry I went over the time allotted," the speaker apologized. "I looked for a clock, but this room doesn't seem to have one."

The ever-helpful heckler had a comment. "You didn't see the *calendar* by the door?"

SILENCE OF THE P.A.M.

During the question period after a lecture by the great mathematical physicist Paul Adrien Maurice Dirac, someone stood up and said, "I did not understand your last equation."

Dirac stood there in silence for some moments. Finally the chairman asked, "Professor Dirac, aren't you going to answer that question?"

Dirac looked at the chairman with surprise. "He did not ask a question, he made a statement."

YOU SAY YOU WANT AN EVOLUTION?

Take a simple math problem, subject it to thirty years of new, improved teaching methods, and deduce the formula to yield our average yearly drop in SAT scores.

In 1960: "A logger sells a truckload of lumber for $100. His cost of production is 4/5 of this price. What is his profit?"

In 1970 (traditional math): "A logger sells a truckload of lumber for $100. His cost of production is 4/5 of this price. In other words, $80. What is his profit?"

In 1970 (New Math): "A logger exchanges a set L of lumber for a set M of money. The cardinality of the set M is 100, and each element m∈M is worth $1. Make one hundred dots representing the elements of the set M. The set C of costs of production contains 20 fewer points than the set M. Represent the set C as a subset of M, and answer the following question: what is the cardinality of the set P of profits?"

In 1980: "A logger sells a truckload of wood for $100. His cost of production is $80, and his profit is $20. Your assignment: underline the number 20."

In 1990: "By cutting down beautiful forest trees, a logger makes $20. What do you think of this way of making money? (Topic for class participation: How did the forest birds and squirrels feel?)"

U.S. AND JAPAN: STUDYING IMBALANCE

An American student meets a Japanese student. The Japanese student says: "Every day, I work at my studies for eight hours. I work two hours to please my family, three hours for the honor of the Emperor, and three hours for the glory of Japan. What about you?"

The American says: "Every day I also study two hours to please my family. America has no emperor—and for Japan, why would I work?"

FUNDAMENTALS OF LECTURING

Far too many people give lectures like G-strings—they touch on everything but don't really cover a thing.

Let your lectures instead resemble tennis shorts. Stick close to the subject and cover as much as you can, but not so much that the audience loses interest.

AROMATIC CHEMISTRY GONE WRONG CAN REALLY STINK

Two organic chemists came out of a colleague's seminar shaking their heads. "What a waste of an hour," lamented one. "This latest mechanism of his is absolutely and completely wrong!"

"Well, that's Smith for you," said the other one philosophically. "The guy is always wrong."

"Ha! Smith should be so lucky to be *that* consistent."

CAPSULE SEMINAR REVIEW: IN THIS CASE, A BITTER PILL

The part that was new wasn't true, and the part that was true wasn't new.

AND HE'D DARN WELL BETTER HAVE IT MEMORIZED

What do you do if you need to know a complex chemical formula? Well, a student memorizes it, an assistant professor looks it up in the handbook, and a full professor asks one of his students.

How many science professors does it take to change a light bulb?
Only one,
but he gets three tech reports out of it.
(Alternate answer)
Only one,
but that's assuming he has enough graduate students to do the actual work.

Thesis advisors

THE EARLY ARCHETYPE OF THE THESIS ADVISOR

What is a thesis advisor? A thesis advisor is a revered figure you can go to for advice and assistance, and get . . . advice. There have been thesis advisors much longer than there have been theses, as the following story demonstrates.

Moishe goes to the rabbi in his little shtetl, and says, "My chickens are looking sickly. What must I do?"

RABBI: Feed them oat bran mixed with a little bit of milk.

A week later.

MOISHE: I did what you told me, but now my chickens are looking worse.

RABBI: This time mix together a little molasses and honey, and feed them twice a day.

A week later.

MOISHE: My chickens are really in terrible shape.

RABBI: I'll tell you what. Mash up some bananas for them, with a little wheat flour sprinkled on.

A week later. Moishe comes in looking very sad.

MOISHE: Reb, my chickens have all died.

RABBI: That's too bad. I had a lot of other good ideas.

BY THE WAY, HOW ARE THOSE CHICKENS DOING?

RABBI: On the way over to the shul tonight, I saw an interesting sight—a red herring, hanging from a wall, whistling.

MOISHE: But Reb, herrings aren't red.

RABBI: So, you can't paint a herring red?

MOISHE: But herrings don't hang on walls.

RABBI: You can't with a hammer maybe nail it to a wall?

MOISHE: But Reb, herrings don't whistle.

RABBI: Nu, so they don't whistle!

THE EVEN EARLIER ARCHETYPE OF THE THESIS ADVISOR?

Alexander the Great decided to study geometry so he could survey the extent of his conquests. He explained to Menaechmos that he did not have much time to spare from military duties and had to be taught in the quickest possible way.

"Alas, Your Majesty," sighed Menaechmos, "there is no royal road to geometry."

A-PAULI-ING LACK OF ENTHUSIASM

Wolfgang Pauli (1900–1958), the father of the Pauli Exclusion Principle for electrons, had very exclusive views about who should and should not be accounted a physicist. Young prodigies were the target of his special scorn. "So young, and yet—" he said of one, "—already he has done so little."

This put Pauli's students in an unenviable position. When asked to write a recommendation, Pauli would instead make a list of all the student's faults. There was one student so brilliant, however, that even Pauli could write nothing less than a glowing recommendation, to wit, "I have nothing against this man."

YOU THINK *YOU'VE* GOT A HELPFUL THESIS ADVISOR?

In Munich in the days of the great theoretical physicist Arnold Sommerfeld (1868–1954), trolley cars were cooled in summer by two small fans set into their ceilings. When the trolley was in motion, air flowing over its top would spin the fans, pulling warm air out of the cars. One student noticed that although the motion of any given fan was fairly random—fans could turn either clockwise or counterclockwise—the two fans in a single car nearly always rotated in opposite directions. Why was this? Finally he brought the problem to Sommerfeld.

"That is easy to explain," said Sommerfeld. "Air hits the fan at the front of the car first, giving it a random motion in one direction. But once the trolley begins to move, a vortex created by the first fan travels down the top of the car and sets the second fan moving in precisely the same direction."

"But, Professor Sommerfeld," the student protested, "what happens is in fact the opposite! The two fans nearly always rotate in different directions."

"Ahhhh!" said Sommerfeld. "But of course that is even *easier* to explain."

ILLUSTRATING THE IDEAL CASE, A THESIS ADVISOR WHO KNOWS HOW TO DEAL WITH *DEAD* CHICKENS

A little rabbit was sitting in a field, scribbling on a pad of paper, when a fox came along. "What are you doing, little rabbit?"

"I'm working on my dissertation," said the rabbit.

"Really?" said the fox. "And what is your topic?"

"Oh, the topic doesn't matter," said the rabbit.

"No, tell me," begged the fox.

"If you must know," said the rabbit, "I'm advancing a theory that rabbits can eat many quite large animals—including, for instance, foxes."

"Surely you have no experimental evidence for that," scoffed the fox.

"Yes, I do," said the rabbit, "and if you'd like to step inside this cave for a moment I'll be glad to show you." So the fox followed the rabbit into the cave. About half an hour passed. Then the rabbit came back out, brushing a tuft of fox fur off his chin, and began once more to scribble on his pad of paper.

News spreads quickly in the forest, and it wasn't long before a curious wolf came along. "I hear you're writing a thesis, little rabbit," said the wolf.

"Yes," said the rabbit, scribbling away.

"And the topic?" asked the wolf.

"Not that it matters, but I'm presenting some evidence that rabbits can eat larger animals—including, for example, wolves." The wolf howled with laughter. "I see you don't believe me," said the rabbit. "Perhaps you would like to step inside this cave and see my experimental apparatus."

Licking her chops, the wolf followed the rabbit into the cave. About half an hour passed before the rabbit came out of the cave with his pad of paper, munching on what looked like the end of a long gray tail.

Then along came a big brown bear. "What's this I hear about your thesis topic?" he demanded.

"I can't imagine why you all keep pestering me about my topic," said the rabbit irritably. "As if the topic made any difference at all."

The bear sniggered behind his paw. "Something about rabbits eating bigger animals was what I heard—and apparatus inside the cave."

"That's right," snapped the rabbit, putting down his pencil. "And if you want to see it I'll gladly show you." Into the cave they went, and a half hour later the rabbit came out again picking his teeth with a big bear claw.

By now all the animals in the forest were getting nervous about the rabbit's project, and a little mouse was elected to sneak up and peek into the cave when the rabbit's back was turned. There she discovered that the mystery of the rabbit's thesis had not only a solution but also a moral. The mystery's solution is that the cave contained an enormous lion. And the moral is that your thesis topic really *doesn't* matter—as long as you have the right thesis advisor.

Thesis Experiments from Hell

ERNEST ENCOURAGEMENT

Ernest Rutherford trained many of the most brilliant physicists of the twentieth century. He strolled around the laboratory, humming "Onward Christian Soldiers" under his breath, urging his students on with a constant litany of "When will you get results? I want you to give me results." Legend had it that one university bricklayer walked off a job in Rutherford's lab with the complaint that some rude old man kept coming up to demand why *he* wasn't getting results.

Rutherford kept students' noses to the grindstone of experiment, and discouraged idle speculation. As for budding theorists they could go elsewhere. Rutherford's battle cry was, "Don't let me catch anyone in *my* laboratory talking about the universe!"

FUNNY, MOSELEY PEOPLE WOULD RATHER WORK WITH RUTHERFORD

In spite of his eagerness for results, late-night suffering in his laboratory was not something Rutherford encouraged. "Go home and think!" was his battle cry to students he caught returning to an experiment after dinner.

His protégé H.J.G. Moseley (1887–1915) had a different philosophy. Sir George Darwin described his youthful experience in Moseley's lab: "There were two rules for his work. First: when you started to set up the apparatus for an experiment you must not stop until it was set up. Second: when the apparatus was set up you must not stop work until the experiment was done." One benefit of working with Moseley: you acquired an unparalleled knowledge of places in Manchester that served food at three in the morning.

SCIENTIFIC REPUTATIONS

"When a scientist doesn't know the answer to a problem, he is ignorant. When he has a hunch as to what the result is, he is uncertain. And when he is pretty darn sure of what the result is going to be, he is in some doubt."

LEE A. DUBRIDGE, FOR MANY YEARS PRESIDENT OF CALTECH

"My dear colleague, for seven years of misfortune I had one moment of good luck."

PAUL EHRLICH, DESCRIBING HIS DISCOVERY OF THE ANTIDOTE
FOR SYPHILIS

"Splitting the atom is like trying to shoot a gnat in the Albert Hall at night and using ten million rounds of ammunition on the off chance of getting it. That should convince you that the atom will always be a sink of energy and never a reservoir of energy."

ERNEST RUTHERFORD, EXPLAINING WHY ATOMIC BOMBS WOULD
NEVER WORK

"One word characterizes the most strenuous of the efforts for the advancement of science that I have made perseveringly during fifty-five years; that word is failure."

LORD KELVIN

(TWO CENTURIES LATER) WHO? WHAT?
The Four Stages of Public Opinion
I (Just after publication)
The novelty is absurd and subversive of Religion and Morality. The propounder both fool & knave.

II (TWENTY YEARS LATER)

The Novelty is absolute Truth and will yield a full & satisfactory explanation of things in general—The propounder a man of sublime genius and perfect virtue.

III (FORTY YEARS LATER)

The Novelty won't explain things in general after all and therefore is a wretched failure. The propounder a very ordinary person advertised by a clique.

IV (A CENTURY LATER)

The Novelty a mixture of truth & error. Explains as much as could reasonably be expected.

The propounder worthy of all honour in spite of his share of human frailties, as one who has added to the permanent possessions of science.

T. H. HUXLEY

AND BESIDES THAT, SCIENTISTS WILL NEVER FORGIVE HIM FOR ALL THE EXECUTION JOKES HE STARTED

After the French Revolution, the chemist Antoine Lavoisier (1743–1794) was declared an enemy of the people and guillotined. "It took only a moment to make this head fall," protested his colleague Joseph-Louis Lagrange, "and a hundred years will perhaps not be enough to produce its like."

But Lavoisier's bad luck did not end with death. In the 1890s France erected a statue to his memory. Soon a scandal arose: the sculptor had reproduced not Lavoisier's face, but that of someone else! Then, during World War II, the statue was melted down for its metal content. It has still not been replaced.

THE EARLY SIGNS OF SCIENTIFIC GREATNESS

Consider Paul Ehrlich (1854–1915), winner of the 1908 Nobel Prize for his discovery of the first cure for syphilis. When Ehrlich was a student at Breslau, he was pointed out to the great Robert Koch as "little Ehrlich. He is very good at staining but he will never pass his examinations."

*   *   *

Young Einstein's father once asked the boy's headmaster what career his son should follow. "It doesn't matter," replied the headmaster. "*He* will never make a success of anything."

Gregor Mendel (1822–1884), the Austrian botanist whose experiments with peas originated the modern science of genetics, never even succeeded in passing the examination to become a high school science teacher. His examiners were satisfied with his knowledge of physics, but flunked him in biology.

Charles Darwin (1809–1882), like many youthful scientists, was not interested in the classical education that was standard fare for British schoolboys throughout the nineteenth century. His neglect of his schoolwork brought down on his head the wrath of his father, who reproached him with these words: "You care for nothing but shooting, dogs, and rat-catching, and you will be a disgrace to yourself and all your family."

BETTER MAYBE HE SHOULD HAVE BEEN A DENTIST

An immigrant who had worked his way up from poverty was very proud of his scientist son at Harvard. When the young man came home all excited about Einstein's theory of relativity, the father asked him to explain it.

"Relativity is like this," explained the scientist-to-be, trying to keep things very simple. "If you are sitting on a hot stove, a minute seems like an hour. If you are kissing a beautiful woman, an hour seems like a minute. It is all relative."

The old man thought about this and scratched his head. "And from this your Mr. Einstein makes a living?"

THAT'S NICE, DEAR. DID YOU FORGET TO PICK UP THE DRY-CLEANING *AGAIN*?

In Francis Crick's autobiography, *What Mad Pursuit*, he tells the following story: After he and James Watson had made their historic discovery of the double-helix structure of DNA, they went across the street to their usual pub to inform the world at large that they had just discovered the secret of life. Crick does not tell us how his fellow-patrons received this information, but he does say that his wife, Odile, told him years later that "You were always coming home and saying things like that, so naturally I thought nothing of it."

ACTUALLY, I WANT TO GO TO SWEDEN AND I CAN'T WAIT

In a hurry to get back to the library, a young scientist-to-be wheeled his overfilled shopping cart into a lane marked "Ten Items or Less." In some places you can get away with stuff like that, but not in Cambridge, Mass. A burly woman with jaw of granite tapped him on the shoulder. "What's your problem here, sonny?" she asked. "You go to Harvard and you can't count, or you go to M.I.T. and you can't read?"

EVEN $E = MC^2$ WAS A MISTAKE, I MEANT TO WRITE MC^3

When Albert Einstein visited Chicago during the 1920s, some graduate students invited him to see their thesis experiments. To one, Einstein ventured a suggestion that the experiment might be done in a slightly different way. Impossible! protested the student. Einstein submitted to a three-minute lecture on all the reasons his plan was unusable, then shook his head. "My ideas are never good," he sighed.

IT'S WHERE THOMSON AND MAXWELL AND CRICK AND WATSON WORKED, THAT'S WHERE!

Cambridge University's great physics laboratory, affectionately known as "the Cavendish," is not named for Henry Cavendish, the eccentric millionaire scientist contemporary with Benjamin Franklin. That eighteenth-century Cavendish, the grandson of the second Duke of Devonshire, lived like a hermit in his magnificent London house while he performed electrical experiments of various kinds. No women were allowed to see him, not even the family servants with whom Cavendish would only communicate by means of notes left on the hall table. When dragged to a reception to meet some distinguished fellow-scientists, Cavendish broke from his escorts and ran away down the corridor squeaking like a bat.

In fact it was Henry's distant kinsman William Cavendish, himself the seventh Duke of Devonshire, who in 1870 gave to Cambridge the £6300 needed to build and equip completely its new physics laboratory.

Cambridge was lucky again in the first person chosen to head the lab: both Lord Kelvin and Helmholtz were offered that first professorship, but declined. Thus it happened that the first man to head the Cavendish was the relatively obscure James Clerk Maxwell, whose Maxwell's equations would soon demonstrate the unity of electricity, magnetism, and light.

The Cavendish remains a name to conjure with for physicists all over the world. Betsy Devine recalls the day in 1982 when she and her husband Frank Wilczek first arrived in Cambridge. "I am going to the Cavendish Laboratory," Frank proudly told the station taxi driver.

"You are?" said the driver. "Is that somewhere in Cambridge?"

NO, *THAT'S* SOMEWHERE IN (THE OTHER) CAMBRIDGE!

Joel Cohen remembers a chat (in Washington, D.C.) about his intention to study mathematics at Harvard.

"Harvard, eh?" said his companion. "Isn't that up around New York?"

WE KNOW SOME DOCTORS WE'D RENAME MICRO-KAN

Robert Andrews Millikan (1868–1953), the Caltech physicist who won the 1923 Nobel Prize for his oil-drop experiment to measure the charge on a single electron, was not always easy to get along with. His massive self-confidence inspired some colleagues to invent a new fundamental constant of nature. The "kan," they said, was the smallest endurable unit of modesty.

Perhaps Millikan was just reacting against his housekeeper's attitude. She is said to have answered the family phone by saying, "Yes, this is Dr. Millikan's house, but he's not the kind of doctor who does anybody any good."

REAL DOCTORS HAVE A CODE OF THEIR OWN, YOU KNOW

Samuel B. Morse (1791–1852), inventor of the telegraph, was as proud of his talent as an artist as of any scientific achievements. One day when a doctor friend came to visit, Morse proudly ushered him to his studio. On the easel was the picture, a portrait of a dying man, he had been laboring on for months. The doctor looked it over but said nothing.

"Well," Morse demanded eagerly, "What do you think?"

The doctor studied the portrait a moment or two, and then gave his conclusion in a single word—"Malaria."

WITH FAME LIKE THIS, ECONOMICS *MUST* BE A SCIENCE

For the centennial of Karl Marx's birth, reporters visited the British Museum where he spent so many years doing the research that culminated in *Das Kapital*.

Wonder of wonders, reporters were able to find an old usher who actually remembered Marx himself. "Yes," said the usher, "Karl Marx. I remember him. He always used to sit in that corner over there, day after day. Then one day he just disappeared—nobody ever heard of him again."

IN ONE HUNDRED WORDS OR LESS . . .

Sir Gavin Rylands De Beer, in his biography of Charles Darwin, quotes the following student's assessment from an actual British A-level exam: "Darwin's theory was based upon three good solid pints [*sic*]; 1. the struggle for exits 2. the survival of the fattest 3. maternal selection."

"I have long discovered that geologists never read each other's works, and that the only object in writing a book is a proof of earnestness."
CHARLES DARWIN

SSSHHH ! WE'RE GETTING READY TO SHOOT THE RUSSIANS FULL OF COSMIC RAYS!

After the Mansfield Amendment was passed, researchers using government money had to submit "proof" that their work was somehow useful to their supporting agency.

A very theoretical physics group at the Lawrence Livermore labs at Berkeley had for years been funded by the Air Force. Still, it turned out no problem to get their grant renewed—scientists are clever people after all. This nettled one brash young member of the group so much that he took it upon himself to write an angry letter to the Air Force, denouncing the hypocrisy of paying for work unrelated to the national defense.

Time passed, the wheels of bureaucracy ground around a few times, and the young man got a letter assuring him that the research of his group was indeed vital to the mission of the Air Force. Completely unconvinced, the angry young man wrote back demanding that they spell out exactly what aspect of *his* research was related to the Air Force in any way. The response: "We're sorry, but that information is classified."

BUT THANKS SO VEDDY MUCH FOR YOUR ENQUIRY

Back in the days when the British government was using wooden signals worked by hand to send long-distance messages, the meteorologist Sir Francis Ronalds (1788–1873) rigged up an electric telegraph on his estate. In order to prove that it could work over substantial distances, he wrapped eight miles of wire around and around his garden. When he offered his idea to the British government, however, they were not interested. "Telegraphs are wholly unnecessary," they told him, "and no other than the one in use will be employed."

The Rewards of Fame

> *"To attempt to live by any scientific pursuit is a farce. A man of science may earn great distinction, but not bread. He will get invitations to all sorts of dinners and conversaziones, but not enough income to pay his cab fare."*
>
> T. H. HUXLEY, IN A LETTER TO HIS FIANCÉE

THIS STUDENT DIDN'T SEE IT FROM THE RIGHT ANGLE

The story is told of Euclid (fl. 300 B.C.) that he began to teach geometry to a wealthy dilettante, who asked him after struggling through the First Proposition, "What will I gain from learning this?"

Euclid sent for his servant at once and had him present the student with a copper coin, "since," he said, "this man must make some profit out of everything he learns."

> *"I cannot afford to waste my time making money."*
>
> LOUIS AGASSIZ, REFUSING TO GO ON A LECTURE TOUR

"Well, I wasn't using the money. I imagine someone must now be getting something out of it."
GEORGE WASHINGTON CARVER, ON LEARNING THAT THE BANK WITH HIS LIFE'S SAVINGS IN IT HAD FAILED

SCIENCE OF ENTERTAINING ANGELS

The archangel Gabriel appeared before a scientist, presumably a very, very good one, maybe Agassiz or Carver. "Professor, I have come to grant your dearest wish. Which do you choose—infinite wealth, infinite wisdom, or infinite beauty?"

A scientist doesn't think long about such choices. "Infinite wisdom." POOOFFF!!! The scientist blinked, then sighed a sigh full of infinite wisdom. "Damn! So I should have taken the money."

The Science of the Sneer

M. LE MARQUIS GETS PASTEURIZED

One of Louis Pasteur's early discoveries was that certain diseases of silkworms could be avoided by using only germ-free breeding stock. One noble silkworm breeder who scoffed at Pasteur received this withering reply: "I want to tell you, Monsieur le Marquis, that you don't know the first thing about my investigations and their results, about the definite principles they have established and their practical applications. Most of them you have not read and the ones that have come to your attention you did not understand."

TAKING A HARD LINUS

Two-time Nobelist Linus Pauling's enthusiasm for high doses of vitamin C won little support from doctors. One clinical test Pauling liked to cite showed that skiers who ingested a gram of vitamin C daily had 60 percent fewer upper respiratory infections. "I am not impressed by that paper," an eminent physician said to Pauling.

Retorted Pauling, "I am not impressed by your saying you are not impressed by that paper."

PRAISING A COLLEAGUE WITH FAINT DAMNS

"Al's research may not amount to much—but you have to consider the quality of his teaching."

"Gee, I never heard Al was anything great as a teacher."

"In fact—he's not."

INSULTS I'M GLAD I DIDN'T COME UP WITH

In 1962, when Rachel Carson (1907–1964) published *Silent Spring*, an indictment of the careless use of pesticides, many efforts were made to discredit her. One major producer of DDT accused her of something that, thanks to the ecology movement that grew up in the wake of her book, no longer sounds like such an insult. He charged her with being "a fanatic defender of the balance of nature."

SCIENTIFIC WRITING ON THE WALLS

SCIENCE GRAFFITI AND SOCIAL SCIENCE GRAFFITI
There are only two kinds of scientists—
social scientists and antisocial scientists.

If a subject has "science" in its name—it isn't.

WHAT PHYSICISTS SCRAWL ON THE WALLS OF THEIR HALLS
Heisenberg *may* have been here.
Nuclear physics $\cong$ unclear physics
Solid state $\cong$ squalid state

UNBOUNDED MATHEMATICAL GRAFFITI
Why did the mathematician name his dog Cauchy?
Because he left a residue at every pole.

Why is it that the more accuracy you demand from an interpolation
function, the more expensive it is to compute?
That's the Law of Spline Demand

$$\lim_{x \to 8+} \frac{1}{x-8} = +\infty$$

$$\lim_{x \to 5+} \frac{1}{x-5} = +\text{5}$$

Analysts do it continuously.
Algebraists do it discretely
(but in groups).

Topologists do it with characteristic class.
Topologists don't even differentiate.

MORE MATHEMATICIANS CLAIM TO DO IT—AND HOW!
Probabilists, we're not sure if they do it.
Logicians do it consistently.
Differential Topologists do it smoothly.
Algebraic Topologists do it manifold ways.
Group Theorists simply do it.
Software Engineers do it with user-friendly I/O.
Pythagoras did it first.
Markov did it with chains.
Fermat did it, but can't prove it.
Norbert Wiener did it prodigiously.
Gauss did it better than anyone.

ROBERT J. LIPSHUTZ

WARNING SIGN OUTSIDE THE INSTITUTE FOR SEX RESEARCH
Trespassers will be violated.

There are two kinds of scientific fact—
those that support your views 100 percent
and those that are *very* hard to interpret.

In God We Trust—all others must show data.

SIGN OF THE TIMES (ON THE DOOR OF A CHEMICAL STOCKROOM)
Please do not smoke.
If you must light up, please exit as quickly as possible
through the large hole that will appear in the roof.

MEDICAL SCIENCE

Capsule Medical History

FEARING A PLAGUE ON *ONE* OF THEIR HOUSES

William Harvey (1578–1657), physician to Charles I and discoverer of the circulation of the blood, left England to study medicine in Padua at the time Galileo was there teaching mathematics. Harvey's work played a major role in the movement to base the sciences on experiment and observation, instead of on slavish adherence to authority in general and Aristotle in particular. Harvey himself admired Aristotle, and considered that most writers on medicine were mere "shit-breeches" by comparison.

Traveling to Venice in 1636, Harvey was stopped by authorities who feared he might be coming from a region infected with plague. Stranded in Treviso until his papers could be investigated, Harvey proved himself an early instinctive pioneer of germ theory when he chose a drafty cow shed over the more comfortable resting place he was offered by town worthies—their plague hospital!

BESIDES, I DISTINCTLY HEARD HIM SAY "SEND IN THE BLOODY SURGEON!"

Back in the days when a surgeon's blood-stained coat was the proud emblem of his expertise, Astley Cooper (1768–1841) was called in to cut a wen from the scalp of King George IV. Inquiring later why the king had seemed displeased, he learned the king was annoyed he had operated without putting on a clean shirt or even washing his hands.

"God bless me!" exclaimed Cooper, looking down at his hands and shirt, both well-spattered with gore. "The King, sir, is so very particular."

MAKING SURGERY AN ETHER-OR PROPOSITION

Surgical anesthetics (the word was coined by Oliver Wendell Holmes) were first used in the United States. It was a Connecticut dentist named William Thomas Green Morton (1819–1868) who first demonstrated the use of ether. Because he hoped to patent his process, he tried to disguise the ether by mixing it with dye and perfume. The news of a successful operation to remove a tubercular gland from the neck of a housepainter anesthetized with ether reached England late in 1846, and the first British attempt followed shortly thereafter.

It was not attempted without some skepticism. "We are going to try a Yankee dodge today, gentlemen," announced the surgeon Robert Liston (1794–1847), "for making men insensible." His final comment, after amputating the leg of a butler named Frederick Churchill was more enthusiastic: "This Yankee dodge, gentlemen, beats mesmerism hollow."

SURGICAL TRIPLE THREAT

Robert Liston operated with great theatrical flourish and a speed that impressed and dismayed more cautious colleagues. In the days before anesthetics, speed was important—but to operate at Liston's breakneck pace created certain other risks. One unfortunate gentleman who arrived to have his leg amputated (an operation Liston boasted took him no more than three minutes) departed minus both leg and testicles.

Liston's most famous amputation is neither that nor the first British operation under ether. To continue with negatives, the case is not famous for its speed—though the patient's leg came off in less than two and a half minutes—nor for its success—the patient died of hospital gangrene.

Sad to say, Liston's assistant died of gangrene from the same surgical knife—in his enthusiasm for speed, the great surgeon lopped off the poor man's fingers. But that is not all. Undeterred, Liston continued to wield his scalpel with such panache that he slashed through the coattails of a distinguished spectator, who promptly dropped dead of fright.

Dr. Richard Gordon in his book *Great Medical Disasters* describes the affair as "the only operation in history with a 300% mortality rate."

THE LUSTER OF LISTER

Joseph Lister (1827–1912), the famous pioneer of antiseptic surgery, was also a dedicated teacher to generations of medical students. "Never ask a patient if he has had syphilis," he admonished his students. "If you know your work, there will be no need to do so, and why add to the poor fellow's transgressions by tempting him to tell a lie? Surely he has done enough wrong already."

Lister's belief that many surgical complications were caused by germs was not universally accepted by his contemporaries. "Where are the germs?" demanded Dr. J. Hughes Bennett, one of Lister's colleagues at Edinburgh. "Show them to us and we will believe. Has anybody seen these germs?"

Another fierce opponent of Lister was George Bernard Shaw, who hated the painful carbolic acid treatment that had been forced on him after foot surgery. "The *fin de siècle* stank of carbolic acid," complained Shaw, and Lister's innovations were nothing but "a disastrous blunder."

Nevertheless, Lister received many honors in his lifetime including, in 1902, the newly created Order of Merit. At his installation ceremony, Edward VII was to place the ribbon holding a jeweled medal around Lister's neck. Lister's biographer, Richard Fisher, reports that, after two efforts, the ribbon proved too small and the medal sat stranded on top of Lister's nose. "I think, sir," he said to the king, "that I had better take it away in my hand."

One honor Lister steadfastly refused. He did not want to be buried in Westminster Abbey, choosing instead to lie next to his wife, Agnes, in West Hampstead Cemetery.

OR MAYBE THE QUEEN, BUT I DON'T RECALL THAT WE PASTEUR

Louis Pasteur's discovery of a cure for rabies made him famous and beloved all over the world, but he remained always very modest. At the International Congress of Medicine held in London in 1861, Pasteur was invited to mount the platform by its president, Sir George Paget (later to be J. J. Thomson's father-in-law). The crowd recognized Pasteur at once, and began to cheer. Pasteur turned to his son-in-law, and said, "Undoubtedly the Prince of Wales has arrived. We should have come sooner."

MEDICAL SCIENCE.... 113

ADMIT THAT ITS CHANCES LOOKED MOLDY

The 1945 Nobel Prize for physiology and medicine was shared by Alexander Fleming, Howard Walter Florey, and Ernst Boris Chain "for the discovery of penicillin and its therapeutic effect for the cure of different infectious maladies." In fact it was Fleming who had originally detected the bactericidal effects of *Penicillium* mold, an organism that makes blue streaks in Roquefort cheese. He was unable to get funding to continue his research, however.

Florey and Chain began work on the mold in hopes that a long-term project would save them from having to beg money every year from the eternally hard-pressed Oxford School of Pathology. Deeply in debt, the school had warned its investigators to think long and hard before requesting even a stirring rod. "I don't think the idea of helping suffering humanity ever entered our minds," Florey frankly admitted.

Fortunately, their project was funded solely on the basis of its scientific interest. It later turned out that at least one American biologist had tried to get money to study the therapeutic possibilities of *Penicillium*. The idea that this scientific novelty might actually be useful was considered too far-fetched to be worth a dime.

Medical Practices and Malpractices

ALIVE, BUT *HOW* HAPPY?

A monarch in need of some delicate surgery decided to hold a contest for all the surgeons in his country. After months of trials, the royal chamberlain announced with pride that the kingdom's three top surgeons had been selected. The third-best would be first to show his skill.

The door opened to admit a handsome man of about forty, wearing a spotless lab coat on top of his Brooks Brothers suit. From one pocket of his lab coat he produced a small vial, and from the other he drew a scalpel. "Your Majesty," he said respectfully, "this vial contains a specimen of *Drosophila*. And, if your Majesty will permit . . ." He uncorked the vial, and a tiny fruit fly flew out. Instantly, the surgeon's scalpel flourished through the air, and the fly dropped to the floor in two precisely equal pieces.

"Marvelous!" cried the king. "Give this man a bag of gold, and then send in the *second*-best surgeon to me."

The second-best surgeon, a distinguished woman of fifty, arrived in a green surgical scrub suit and attended by white-robed assistants. "Your Majesty," she said politely, "I also have brought a specimen of *Drosophila*." As she spoke, one nurse handed her a gilt-handled scalpel and the other unscrewed the lid of a sterile specimen jar to release the fruit fly. Before it had flown more than a foot, it dropped to the floor in four precisely equal pieces.

The king was so delighted he awarded her two bags of gold. Now it was time for the very best surgeon of all to make an appearance. The door opened once more, and through it appeared a scruffy young person of indeterminate sex, wearing a grubby lab coat and carrying a crumpled paper bag. "Who the hell are you?" demanded the indignant king.

"Your Majesty, I have the honor to be the very best surgeon in your entire kingdom. I have come to demonstrate my skill on this bag full of fruit flies." While the king looked on skeptically, the newcomer pulled a small scalpel from his pocket and opened the bag, releasing a cloud of fruit flies. For two or three minutes the scalpel flashed among the fruit flies, then the surgeon stood back with a satisfied smile and indicated the still busy cloud of flies.

"So what is this?" demanded the king. "Every one of those flies is still alive!"

"Alive and happy. But, the males are now *circumcised*, your Majesty!"

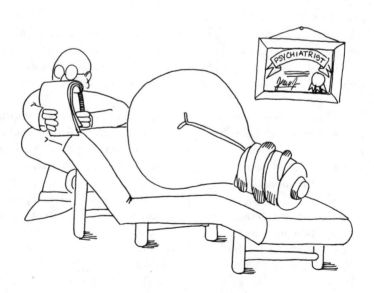

WORLD'S BRIGHTEST LIGHT BULB JOKES FOR DOCTORS

How many premed students does it take to change a light bulb?
*Five. One to change the bulb and the other four
to pull the ladder out from under him.*

How many doctors does it take to change a light bulb?
That depends—does this bulb have health insurance?

How many psychiatrists does it take to change a light bulb?
Only one, but that bulb has got to want *to change.*

How many neurosurgeons does it take to change a light bulb?
*Just one. He raises the light bulb into position
and then the universe revolves around him.*

DOC, WHY ARE *YOU* HOLDING YOUR HEAD?

"Doctor, I'm so miserable I don't know what to do. I get the most terrible headaches and nothing will stop them. I've tried every pill known, acupuncture, massage, hypnosis—and nothing works. What now?"

The doctor sadly shook his head. "You have exhausted the resources of conventional medicine. But there is one suggestion I could make. This isn't at all scientific, but it is something that works for me, if you would care to try it."

"Anything, Doctor, just tell me!"

"Well, when I get a headache, I find that it will often go away if I just go home and make love to my wife." So the patient went off with new hope in his eye and the doctor, who was a busy specialist, did not see him again for several months.

But then, what a change had occurred! The patient, once pale and depressed, now looked healthy and robust. He gripped the doctor's hand and shook it fervently. "Doc, how can I ever thank you? That cure worked like a charm. I hope you don't mind if I give some advice in return. You and your wife ought to buy a better mattress."

THE DOCTOR HAVING NOT ONLY A NEW MATTRESS BUT A WHOLE 'NOTHER ATTITUDE

Another sufferer from migraines went to a famous headache specialist. The doctor examined him thoroughly before saying, "I'm afraid your case is unusually difficult. There is one way, and only one, that I could give you some relief."

"What is it, doc? Anything, I swear it."

"Don't be too quick to say that until you hear the remedy. It is," the doctor paused dramatically, "castration."

Well, this changed the man's mind pretty quickly, and he decided to try to live with the headaches or find another cure. But as months dragged on and the headaches got worse, he changed his mind at last. The operation proceeded without a hitch. The patient was soon able to resume his normal routine, his headaches gone but his spirits very low.

One day as he was passing a large department store, it occurred to him that maybe some new clothes would cheer him up. No sooner had he entered the men's department than an elderly salesman came over and took his arm. "You want some new clothes to make you feel better, don't you?" he asked.

The patient was amazed. "How do you know that?"

"How do I know? I've been selling men's clothing for thirty-five years is how I know! How do I know just by looking at you that your shirt size is 32/16?"

"That's right!"

"And your size in a sportcoat is 38 short, am I right?"

"You are! Gee, that's amazing."

"And you always wear jockey shorts, 34 waist."

"No, afraid not. I wear size 30 jockey shorts."

"Size 30?" said the old man. "Why, a man your size wearing jockey shorts that tight, don't they give you migraine headaches?"

MAYBE THE DOCTOR COULD OFFER A PACKAGE DEAL

A doctor has a new and enthusiastic nurse. The first patient of the day shows up with a sprained ankle. "Just take off your clothes and wait in here," she tells him.

"But it's just my ankle—"

"The doctor will examine you shortly. Now undress and get into this robe." So the patient shrugs, strips down, and puts on the robe.

A couple of minutes later, in walks another guy in a robe. "Is this where we wait for the doctor?" he asks. "Hey, can you believe that nurse? My throat is sore, I tell her, but does she listen?"

Their conversation is cut short by the arrival of a third man in a robe, carrying his clothes under one arm and a big cardboard box under the other. "Hey, listen to this," the first patient says. "I got a sprained ankle, this fella has a sore throat, but does the nurse listen? No! Get undressed, she says. You ever hear anything like it?"

The third man scowls at them both. "You think you got problems?" he asks. "I came to deliver this box!"

BAD LUCK TO BE BORN WITH A MODEL T RUNNING BOARD

"Mr. Hilbert, I have some good news and some bad news," the doctor said to his elderly patient. "The good news is, everything wrong with you can be corrected by a simple transplant operation."

"Wonderful, doc! But what's the bad news?"

The doctor shrugged. "The part you need, nobody makes it anymore."

THE GOOD, THE BAD, AND THE GORGEOUS

"Mr. Jones, I'm afraid I have both good news and bad news. The bad news is, you have only a month to live."

"Bad news? That's terrible news! What's the good news?"

"Well, you noticed my new receptionist as you came in? The redhead, with beautiful legs and big blue eyes?"

"Yes?"

"And her *figure*! Amazing—you must have noticed!"

"Yes, doctor, I did. But, what's the good news?"

The doctor leaned forward and whispered, "Tonight, we have a date."

THE WORSE NEWS IS THAT MY AUTOMATIC REDIAL WILL BE BILLING YOUR WIDOW BY THE HOUR

A doctor phoned his patient with some important information. "Mr. Appleby, I have some good news and some bad news. The good news is that you have only twenty-four hours to live."

"I have twenty-four hours to live and that's the good news? What the hell is the bad news?"

"The bad news is that I've been trying to reach you since yesterday."

INTERN-AL COMPLAINT

The young intern sighed. She had already been warned about Mr. Smith's hypochondria—his medical history listed enough ailments for an entire hospital full of patients. And as for symptoms, well, every single one the doctor asked about it, darned if he didn't have it.

Finally the exasperated intern had had enough. "Well, Mr. Smith," she said, "from everything you tell me, we can just skip this physical and get ready for the autopsy."

SELF-DIAGNOSIS AT A GLANDS

"Doctor, doctor, I've got hyperparathyroidism!"

"Calm yourself, my good man. If you were indeed hyperparathyroid, you would have no symptoms at all."

"Exactly why I'm so worried! I *have* no symptoms at all!"

BUT WHAT WOULD THE FAMILY THINK OF HIS GRAVESIDE MANNER?

A policeman summoned to a graveyard late one night arrested a man whose papers showed him to be a respected urologist. "But officer," the doctor protested, "I was fulfilling the last request of a treasured colleague. We promised each other that whoever died first, the other would sprinkle a bottle of bourbon over his grave."

The policeman gave the doctor an angry look. "But that's not what I caught you doing, was it, doctor?"

"But officer—out of the sheerest respect for our mutual calling I filtered the bourbon through my kidneys!"

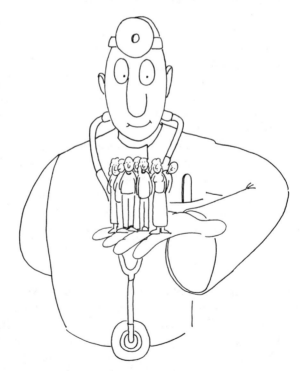

Pediatrician: a doctor with little patients.

Optimist: someone who makes out a duty roster in ink.

What's the difference between a surgeon and an internist?
A surgeon treats fewer patients for more money.

---

and the question is:
What's the difference between a doctor and a preacher?

and the answer is:
A preacher tries to get you into heaven
and a doctor tries to keep you out!

GETTING READY TO SCREW IN LIGHT BULBS WITH HEALTH
INSURANCE?

The med school experience has been described as follows: On the first day of classes you look around you at all the valedictorians, the class presidents, and the twenty-year-old geniuses, and you say to yourself, "What am I doing here?"

After a few months, you look at these same students and ask yourself, "What are they doing here?"

PUBLISH OR PERISH

Not all mathematicians are loners. The number theorist Paul Erdös especially is a very prolific collaborator—so much so that at one time every mathematician could tell you his "Erdös number."

Your Erdös number was assigned by a straightforward method. If you had written a paper with Erdös then your Erdös number was one. If you had not written a paper with Erdös, but had collaborated with someone whose Erdös number was one, then your Erdös number was two, and so on. But in the 1940s, it was rare to find an established mathematician with an Erdös number higher than two. (Erdös himself has Erdös number zero.)

Stefan Bergman is another mathematician well known for writing a lot of papers with other people. Bergman worked at M.I.T. but he had an apartment near Harvard Square, so he used to ride the bus to work every day. Rumor had it that by the end of his first year there, he and the bus driver published two joint papers!

FILE THIS UNDER "N" FOR NIGHTMARE

One day a math department chairman was approached with a very delicate problem. Two years before, a distinguished professor in his department had been sent a young Dr. X's manuscript to review—the manuscript had never been returned. It was the only copy in existence (these were the days before computers) of a long and complex proof. Could the chairman please see if he could find the manuscript?

Very, very tactfully, the chairman got permission to search his colleague's office. Every flat surface was piled high with papers. File cabinets and desk drawers were overflowing with unlabeled folders, though some bore unnerving titles like "Unopened Mail from 1967."

Finally after hours of patient searching he found an unopened envelope two years old that proved to contain a paper by Dr. X. The chairman raced to the phone to report his triumph. The young author asked him to describe the paper, then sighed. "No, that's the wrong one."

TO A YOUNG SCIENTIST

If you want to get published, then heed this advice:
Cite your friends at least once and your enemies twice,
The editor three times, yourself at least four,
And write in a style that's intended to bore.
If you want to get published, here's what you must do
Above all: don't come up with anything new.

J.E.C.

I DON'T LIKE HIS TYPE

Two long-time collaborators were burning the midnight oil in the lab they shared—trying to perfect their synthesis of a complex chemical compound. Suddenly, through one of those rare accidents that characterize experimental science, they stumbled onto a radically new discovery.

One of the two at once raced across the lab to his terminal and started typing furiously.

"Hey," said his colleague, "what's the hurry? We're years ahead of our competitors. There's not a chance those other guys will beat us into print."

"Those other guys?" mumbled the first scientist. "No, I just have to beat you."

JUST WRITE UP THE HOLE THING ERE YOU CASH IN YOUR CHIPS

"So, Professor Murphy, what are you working on these days?" a brash young physicist asked his chairman.

"A bit of writing," said Murphy, trying to look modest without much success. "Now that I'm getting along in years, I decided it was time to try to put everything I know about semiconductors down on paper."

"Great idea. It's so easy to get published with a really short article."

KAC'S THEORY OF PUBLISHABILITY

Suppose you have a statement that is true.
In the best possible world, you can prove it and you understand it.

If you can prove it, but you *don't* understand it,
you can still publish it in a mathematics journal.

If you understand it but you can't prove it,
you can publish it in a physics journal.

If you don't understand it *and* you can't prove it,
you can publish it in an engineering journal.

COHEN'S COROLLARY

If you have a statement that you can't prove, and you
don't understand it,
and moreover it isn't true,
you can publish it in a mathematical biology journal.

NEWMAN'S ADDENDUM

Where can you publish a statement that you can't prove,
that you don't understand,
that isn't true,
and that has been published before by someone else?
In any newspaper.

Scientific Product Warning Labels*

WARNING: This Product Attracts Every Other Piece of Matter in the Universe, Including the Products of Other Manufacturers, with a Force Proportional to the Product of the Masses and Inversely Proportional to the Square of the Distance Between Them.

HANDLE WITH EXTREME CARE: This Product Contains Minute Electrically Charged Particles Moving at Velocities in Excess of Five Hundred Million Miles Per Hour.

ADVISORY: There Is an Extremely Small but Nonzero Chance

* by Susan Hewitt and Edward Subitsky

That, Through a Process Known as "Tunneling," This Product May Spontaneously Disappear from Its Present Location and Reappear at Any Random Place in the Universe, Including Your Neighbor's Domicile. The Manufacturer Will Not Be Responsible for Any Damages or Inconvenience That May Result.

THIS IS A 100% MATTER PRODUCT: In the Unlikely Event That This Merchandise Should Contact Antimatter in Any Form, a Catastrophic Explosion Will Result.

NOTE: The Most Fundamental Particles in This Product Are Held Together by a "Gluing" Force About Which Little Is Currently Known and Whose Adhesive Power Can Therefore Not Be Permanently Guaranteed.

ATTENTION: Despite Any Other Listing of Product Contents Found Hereon, the Consumer is Advised That, in Actuality, This Product Consists of 99.9999999999% Empty Space.

COMPONENT EQUIVALENCY NOTICE: The Subatomic Particles (Electrons, Protons, etc.) Comprising This Product Are Exactly the Same in Every Measurable Respect as Those Used in the Products of Other Manufacturers, and No Claim to the Contrary May Legitimately Be Expressed or Implied.

IMPORTANT NOTICE TO PURCHASERS: The Entire Physical Universe, Including This Product, May One Day Collapse Back into an Infinitesimally Small Space. Should Another Universe Subsequently Re-emerge, the Existence of This Product in That Universe Cannot Be Guaranteed.

EXPERIMENTAL APPARATUS

THERE'S Na BUSINESS LIKE SODIUM BUSINESS

The American physicist R. W. Wood (1868–1955) was a brilliant experimentalist. Fish-eye lenses, improvements in color photography, and a revolution in diffraction gratings came out of his researches on the spectrum of sodium vapor. During his early years at Johns Hopkins, Wood also involved himself in another kind of sodium wizardry.

The route from Wood's laboratory to his boarding house led through a rather rough section of Baltimore. Wood developed an ingenious way to make sure he could pass through unmolested.

Every now and again, Wood used to carry a lump of sodium hidden in a small tin box. As he passed by a crowd of loafers, he would ostentatiously spit into the gutter, just as he dropped in his sodium pellet. Bang! Metallic sodium, when brought into contact with water, bursts into flame with a loud explosion, emitting yellow sparks and clouds of steam. None of the locals *ever* bothered Wood during his late-night rambles!

REALLY, MY DEAR RAYLEIGH

During a visit to England in 1904, Wood became fast friends with another great experimental physicist of his era, John William Strutt, the third Baron Rayleigh (1842–1919). Invited to spend some time at Lord Rayleigh's country house, Wood arrived en route to Cambridge where he was to give some demonstrations. So, in addition to his ordinary baggage, he had with him a large suitcase full of experimental apparatus: glass tubes of various sizes, bits of dirty-looking rubber, and a Bunsen burner he had made himself from a length of old iron pipe, wrapped up in assorted rags.

But in a proper English country house, your luggage is unpacked for you by a valet. When Wood finished chatting with his host and strolled upstairs to dress for dinner, he found to his horror that all his assortment of hardware, rubber, and laboratory glass had been laid in neat rows on top of his dressing table next to his comb and brush. As for the dirty rags of last year's underwear, he found them tidily folded and put away in a lower drawer of the bureau.

WHAT A CARBON DIOXIDE BALLOON LENS ITSELF TO

One of Lord Rayleigh's most intriguing demonstrations grew from his discovery that one could focus sound waves as well as light waves. Rayleigh used a balloon filled with carbon dioxide as a "lens" to concentrate the sound of a pocket watch. A listener standing too far off to hear Rayleigh's watch would suddenly hear it ticking when the balloon was correctly placed between them. The effect could be made intermittent when Rayleigh set the balloon gently swaying back and forth.

HOW NOT TO SET LONDON ABUZZ

In the spring of 1911, Wood and Rayleigh went together to hear Guglielmo Marconi (1874–1937) give one of the popular Friday lectures at London's Royal Institution. This promised to be a historic occasion, as Marconi had announced that his audience would hear transatlantic signals sent through the air from Nova Scotia. In 1911, many people still doubted that "wireless telegraphy" was possible across such distances.

Marconi's assistants worked for days setting up his apparatus. The receiving antennae were mounted on great kites to be flown from the roof. At the climax of his lecture, Marconi was to close the switch and the audience would hear the buzzing of spark discharge set off by coded signals from across the ocean.

Unfortunately, during the course of Marconi's lecture the wind slowly died and the kites all came down, making his demonstration impossible. Wood's biographer, William Seabrook, reports that Rayleigh and Wood were far from impressed. Rayleigh's comment to Wood: "I feel disposed to think that if you or I had required something for a lecture that would make a buzz-buzz we could have accomplished it with simpler apparatus—and we'd have had the buzz-buzz."

A SALESMAN'S UNBREAKABLE PROMISE

The salesman's new line of completely unbreakable glassware sounded so intriguing that the whole chemistry department showed up for his demonstration. First, he took a large Erlenmeyer flask and threw it on the floor. It bounced several times before rolling to a standstill. Then he smacked a graduated cylinder against the edge of a table. It rang like a bell but stayed in one piece. He dropped a handful of pipettes on the floor and stamped all over them with his hobnailed boots. They were unharmed.

"Now, for my final demonstration!" said the salesman. He took a glass stirring rod and bent it nearly double. Suddenly, it snapped. Without missing a beat, he continued, "Ladies and gentlemen, let us examine this unbreakable glass in cross-section."

CASTING SOME LIGHT ON THE N-RAY SPECTRUM

Around the turn of the century, when x-rays and ultraviolet light were still brand-new discoveries, the French academician René-Prosper Blondlot (1849–1930) announced that he too had discovered a new kind of radiation that he called N-rays. These rays seemed to have very complicated properties, and soon all kinds of papers poured out of Blondlot's lab—the problem was that almost no one outside that lab could detect the rays at all. The great American experimentalist R. W. Wood was asked to look into the matter.

The problem, Blondlot explained, was that N-rays were sensitive to a thousand influences of every kind. Inexperienced workers could hardly hope to produce or detect them. He invited Wood to a public demonstration of his own apparatus, to make clear to him some of the difficulties involved.

Blondlot's main apparatus was an N-ray spectroscope he had constructed with lenses and a prism all made of aluminum instead of glass. Blondlot would turn a dial to rotate the prism while his assistant read off the intensity of the N-ray beam focused on a screen. Time and again Blondlot rotated the prism and the assistant read off wavelengths of the transmitted beam—the emission spectrum seemed to be completely reproducible. As a final confirmation, and to make the measurements even more precise (N-rays were sensitive to ordinary light) Blondlot repeated his dial-twiddling with the lights turned off, again with identical results.

Then the lights came back on. In the front row, R. W. Wood sat wordlessly, just holding up for everyone to see the aluminum prism he had removed in the middle of Blondlot's demonstration.

PROOF THAT WOOD'S STRENGTH WAS AS THE STRENGTH OF TEN
*"It requires one genius to formulate one hypothesis that is sound.
It requires ten to nail one that is unsound in its coffin."*
                                                    ERNEST RUTHERFORD

IT'S NOT EASY BEING GREEN!
BOTANY DEPARTMENT CHAIRMAN: So what are you up to these days?
GRAD STUDENT: I'm growing algae on asphalt shingles.
BOTANY DEPARTMENT CHAIRMAN: No wonder research costs are through
   the roof!

THE MAINFRAME THAT DIED AT MIDNIGHT
   A certain military installation had a very expensive computer that
suddenly began to crash on a regular basis. The computer's manufacturers sent in team after team of specialists, but none could figure
out what was going wrong. The crashes occurred only at night, and
while the specialists were there the machine worked perfectly.
   Finally, the general in charge of the building ordered his most
trusted major to stay up all night and see what happened to trigger the

crash. The major sat patiently by the computer and waited. For two nights, nothing went wrong. On the third, just after midnight, a janitor came with a large electric floor polisher. Giving a friendly nod to the watching major, the janitor walked to the big electrical outlet near the door and pulled out the computer's plug so he could plug in his own machine.

Here was the cause of the computer's midnight crashes! It was easy enough to tell the janitor he'd have to find some other source of power. But explaining such idiocy to the general—that would be another matter.

The major solved his problem with brilliant tact—and honesty as well. "I can assure you it won't happen again, sir," he reported. "All it turned out to be was a buffer problem."

THE INTERNATIONAL
SCIENTIFIC COMMUNITY

THINKING FAST ENOUGH BUT NOT BELFAST ENOUGH

For some reason, they decided to hold an international scientific convention in Belfast. And late one evening, a participant was heading back toward his hotel when his worst nightmare came true. From a dark alley, a voice called out, "Hey! What religion are you?"

The scientist thought for a minute. "If I say I'm a Catholic," he reasoned, "that guy in the shadows will probably turn out to be a Protestant. And if I say I'm a Protestant, he'll probably be Catholic." So he shouted back, "I'm Jewish!"

"Ah!" said the voice from the shadows. "I am the luckiest Arab in all of Belfast."

NEXT YEAR IN JERUSALEM, YEAR AFTER NEXT IN BELLEVUE

A scientist at a conference in Jerusalem went to visit the Wailing Wall. It was an impressive sight, with Jews of all ages praying before it. One in particular caught his eye, a distinguished looking gentleman with an enormous gray beard and unusually fine sidelocks. Well, the scientist went to the conference, and at lunch decided to go back to the wall and say a prayer himself.

Imagine his surprise when he saw, among the crowds of people, the same old man he had noticed before. He returned to the conference, and when the afternoon session was over, he went back once more. The old man was still there, davening for all he was worth.

The American could restrain himself no longer. He approached the old man and said, "Truly, your piety amazes me. Have you been praying all day?"

"Yes, my son," said the old man. "I have."

"Do you mind—may I ask what you are praying for?"

"In the morning, my son, I pray for peace in the Middle East—not only for Jews, but Arabs and Christians as well. Then in the afternoon, I pray for peace among nations not only in the Middle East but throughout the world. Then, as the shadows begin to lengthen, I pray not only for political peace but for love and brotherhood to spring up in the hearts of all men everywhere."

The American was nearly weeping, he was so touched by the old man's goodness. "How does it feel to be offering God such holy prayers!"

The old man shrugged. "How does it feel? I'll tell you how it feels. Like I'm facing a blank wall here is how it feels."

Fast-moving Polish Jokes for Scientists

BUT HIS ARGUMENT WAS THE RIGHT ONE

The Aeroflot plane en route to Warsaw ran into heavy turbulence, and was pitching dangerously from side to side. Suddenly, one of the passengers leaped up and shouted, "Everyone with a Polish passport—move to the left side of the aircraft!" People obeyed him, and they landed safely. Why? He had achieved stability by putting all the Poles in the left half-plane.

HYPOTHESIS: LECH WALESA WOULD LIKE HIM

On board a train speeding toward Warsaw, four strangers were sharing one compartment: a Russian officer, a beautiful maiden, an old peasant woman, and a patriotic Polish professor of logic.

For mile upon mile they traveled in silence.

Suddenly—the train had entered a tunnel—darkness fell. And the silence was broken by the sound of a kiss, quite loud, followed by the sound, even louder, of a slap. As the train roared out of the tunnel, the Russian officer had a rueful expression and one cheek much redder than the other. Still no one spoke. But what were they thinking?

The old woman was thinking, "That filthy Russian—she gave him what he deserved!"

The Russian was thinking, "How unfair! That Pole steals a kiss and *I'm* the one she slaps."

The maiden was thinking, "Strange—why did the Russian officer kiss that old woman?"

The logician was thinking, "Oh, what a clever Polish patriot I am! The darkness falls—I kiss my hand—I slap a Russian officer—and no one is the wiser!"

From Russia with Logic

MR. NAPOLEON DIDN'T LIKE THEM EITHER

Yeltsin sent in a squadron of climatologists, but still he couldn't persuade the Ukraine. Get out from under the domination of Moscow, the separatists claim, and Ukrainians will never again have to suffer through one of Russia's freezing winters.

OLD RUSSIAN SAYING (WE HOPED GORBACHEV WOULD CHANGE THE SIGN)

Today is an average day—worse than yesterday, but better than tomorrow.

BUT THE SOVIET VICTORY REMAINS UNCHANGED

TELEPHONE CALLER: Is it true that Ivan Ivanovich has achieved cold fusion in his laboratory at the Landau Institute?

PRAVDA: Yes, the story is true—except for some minor details. It was not at the Landau Institute, but at Dubna. And it was not Ivan Ivanovich, but Piotr Piotrovich. And he did not achieve cold fusion, he emigrated to Israel.

AND PERESTROIKA HAS NOT IMPROVED THE PILE

In the interests of scientific agriculture, the Politburo sent a loyal agronomist to tour a large cooperative farm near Moscow. "How is the potato crop, Comrade?" she asked the group leader.

"Well, Comrade," was his reply, "if you put all our potatoes in one pile they would reach from your foot to the eye of God."

"Comrade," she said angrily, "this is the Soviet Union, and there is no God."

"Of course this is the Soviet Union," said the farmer. "There are no potatoes either."

OLD RUSSIAN STORY HEARD AT MANY A CONFERENCE

An exiled scientist was strolling across the Siberian tundra when he found a tiny bird nearly frozen to death. He picked up the bird and carried it until he found a large pile of still-smoking yak dung. He stuck the bird into the pile to warm it.

Well, the heat revived the bird and it began to sing. A wolf, hearing the sound, came along and ate the bird.

This tiny story has three separate morals that not only scientists should bear in mind.

1. The one who puts you in the yak dung is not necessarily your enemy.
2. The one who gets you out again is not necessarily your friend.
3. And, if you find yourself in yak dung up to your neck—keep your mouth shut!

WOMEN IN SCIENCE

CLEAR SKIES ON THE PREFEMINIST FRONT

I cannot resist quoting from Charles Darwin's inquiries into cannibalism among the inhabitants of Tierra del Fuego. "Jemmy Button told Matthews a long time since, that in winter they sometimes eat the women:—certain it is the women are in a very small proportion. Yet we could not believe it. But the other day a Sealing Captain said that a Fuegian boy whom he had, said the same thing. On being asked 'Why no eat dogs'? the boy answered 'Dog catch otter:—woman good for nothing: man very hungry.' "

BECAUSE WOMAN'S PLACE IS YOU-KNOW-WHERE . . .

When Johns Hopkins opened its medical school in 1896, strong pressure from women, who had raised most of the money to fund it, forced them to admit three women students. Among these was Florence Sabin (1871–1953), later the first woman ever elected a member of the National Academy of Sciences.

Male students retaliated with constant teasing about the "indelicate" subjects they would have to study. For instance, the morning before a lecture on testing diabetics for sugar in their urine, the three women received matching corsages—of sweet pea!

Unperturbed, the women pinned on the corsages and went to class. The male ringleader came up to Sabin and said scornfully, "I see you girls couldn't figure out our joke."

"Oh, we get the message all right," said Sabin calmly. "But we don't get *corsages* that often."

AND MAN'S PLACE IS IN THE LOCKER ROOM?

One of this century's foremost figures in mathematics is the algebraist Emmy Noether (1882–1935). In the twenties, someone asked Edmund Landau if it was true that Göttingen now had a great woman mathematician. "That Emmy Noether is a great mathematician everyone can attest, but that she is a woman I could not swear," replied Landau, ever the stickler for precision.

Göttingen never made Noether a full professor, despite her stature and the pleas of the mathematics faculty. Such an appointment would have required the consent of the whole faculty, many of whom felt that professorships should be reserved for men alone. David Hilbert's plea to these bigots deserves to be recorded: "But, gentlemen, this is a university, not a bathhouse!"

WHY NOT JUST OUT OF CURIE-OSITY?

Marya Sklodowska (1867–1934) became more famous in later life as Marie Curie, the first person of either sex ever awarded two Nobel Prizes.

From childhood she showed enormous powers of concentration. One day while she studied, her sisters piled up stacks of chairs around her. When she finished the book she was reading, she stood up, still oblivious, and the whole construction tumbled down. "That's stupid," was her only comment.

After many delays caused by family poverty, she entered the Sorbonne in 1891. Even years later she remembered her admiration for Paul Appell, a math professor who enlivened a problem in mechanics with the illustration, "I take the sun, and I throw it." It was in Paris also that she met her future husband, Pierre Curie, whose first gift to her, inscribed "To Mlle. Sklodowska, with the respect and friendship of the author, P. Curie," was an article on electromagnetism.

Honors never meant much to either of the Curies. The Davy Medal awarded to them by the Royal Society of London was given to their small daughter Irène (later to win the Nobel Prize herself with husband Frédéric Joliot-Curie) as a "big gold penny" to play with.

Winning the 1903 Nobel Prize in physics made them unwilling social lions. Invited one evening to dinner at Elysée Palace, official residence of the President of the French Republic, Marie Curie was approached by her hostess and asked if she would like to meet the King of Greece. The scientist shook her head and frankly replied, "I don't see any point to it."

FOOD FOR THOUGHT

OSTRICH EGG? WHAT OSTRICH EGG?
OH, YOU MEAN *THAT* OSTRICH EGG!

American science produced not one but two famous E. B. Wilsons. One of them, the father of Nobel Prize-winning physicist Ken Wilson, was Edwin Bidwell Wilson, a mathematician associated with the Harvard School of Public Health who was for fifty years the editor of the *Proceedings of the National Academy of Sciences.*

This is a story about the Columbia cytologist Edmund Beecher Wilson (1856–1939), discoverer of the X and Y chromosomes in human cells. The largest single cell is the newly fertilized ovum of an ostrich, and Wilson had arranged at great expense to have a freshly laid ostrich egg delivered to his laboratory. Unfortunately, when the egg arrived, Wilson had just left for the train station.

One of Wilson's colleagues was T. H. Morgan (1866–1945), the geneticist who sent a generation of students home through the New York subways carrying milk bottles full of fruit flies. Assuming that his colleague had left town for several days, Morgan decided to cook the egg as a feast for his fellow *Drosophila* biologists. Wilson raced back from the station to discover the egg he was planning to dissect had just been scrambled! It was many years before he forgave Morgan.

RECKLESSLY FLINGING AWAY FIVE PERFECTLY GOOD DIRACS

Cheese was being served as the last course of a dinner party attended by the Diracs. "Do you know," Mrs. Dirac remarked, "this must be so delightful for Paul. He simply adores cheese. He has often said that he would be quite content if I gave him nothing for dinner but bread and wine and cheese."

"Did you ever do it?" someone asked.

"Oh, no," said Mrs. Dirac. "I didn't have the heart."

At this, Dirac looked up. "You didn't have the *cheese*," he said.

A-MAZE-ING BREAKFAST ORDER

Ten o'clock in the morning, and the most junior assistant in the behavior lab was taking orders for the snack bar. "Decaf and a cruller," said Gulick, the top postdoc.

"Just a carton of milk" said Handy, whose thesis had been interacting with his ulcer for the past three months.

"Black coffee, no sugar," said Tsuk, who was going to be up all night again tonight.

That left just the head of the lab to answer, but before she could speak a large rat poked its head out of the maze and loudly squeaked, "I want tea, with milk and lemon."

There was a moment of astonished silence. The rat looked around aggressively and continued, "Does that surprise you, that a rat should ask for tea with milk and lemon?"

"Not at all, not at all," said the head of the lab politely. "It's what I was going to get myself."

MAYBE *HE* SHOULD HAVE WRITTEN ABOUT BUTTERCUPS

Antoine Lavoisier (1743–1794) created a revolution in chemical nomenclature with his rational, methodical approach. His personal life too was run on principles of strict rationality. When only nineteen, he noticed that family mealtimes distracted him from research. So, he chose to subsist on a diet of milk alone, since he could drink milk in his room without interrupting his work.

OH, WHERE IS MOTHER NATURE WHEN YOU WANT HER?

Élie Metchnikoff (1845–1916), 1908 Nobel laureate for the phagocyte theory of immunity, used to spend his childhood allowance bribing friends to sit through his lectures on natural history. Later in life, Metchnikoff had a number of theories that many people would have paid to hear about. For instance, he claimed to do his best experiments when a pretty woman was nearby.

Metchnikoff also came to believe that the human large intestine was a useless evolutionary remnant that actually harmed its possessors. Metchnikoff battled his large intestine by subjecting it to gallon upon gallon of sour milk. Years of this unappetizing diet, containing countless millions of authentic Bulgarian bacteria from villages where people regularly live past a hundred, enabled Metchnikoff to survive to the ripe old age of . . . seventy-one!

DAIRY ANIMAL HUSBANDRY

Two distinguished Cornell alumni, now husband and wife, decided to visit its great agriculture school. Peaceful cows stood blissfully chewing their eternal cuds, unperturbed by the glistening gauges and vials set up to measure every aspect of their lives.

Only the herd's stud bull seemed unhappy, snorting and pawing and pacing back and forth by the gate of his pen. "His ten o'clock cow is late," explained their grad student guide. "Old Bert can tell time just about as well as you or I."

"His ten o'clock cow?" asked Mrs. Alum. "So your bull is capable of performing more than once a day?"

"Oh, yes," said the student. "Once a day? Why, he'd just barely be getting warmed up."

"Hmmm," said Mrs. Alum with a sweet smile toward her husband. "What do you think of that, dear?"

Now Mr. Alum had a question for the student. "I suppose that this bull does all his performing with the same cow every day?"

"Certainly not," said the student. "We bring him a fresh cow every single time."

"Hmmm," said Mr. Alum to his wife. "What do you think of that, dear?"

AN APPLE A MILLENNIUM, AND YOU WON'T HAVE TOO MANY O' 'EM

The Hungarian mathematician Farkas Bolyai (1755–1856) wanted an apple tree planted over his grave to commemorate three apples: those of Eve and of Paris, which made a hell of life on earth, and that of Newton, which raised earth again to the status of a heavenly body.

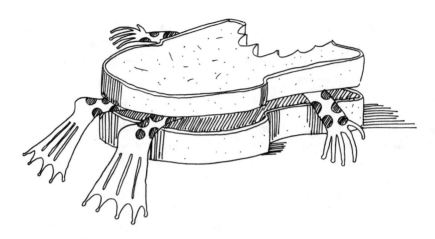

I THOUGHT THAT GUACAMOLE WAS KIND OF CRUNCHY

"Now, class," said the absent-minded biology professor, "I have partially dissected this frog as a demonstration of the proper technique." He pulled a crumpled paper bag from his desk drawer and opened it. Out tumbled three carrot sticks, a sandwich, and a brownie. "Gee, that's funny," said the prof. "I could have sworn I ate my lunch already."

POPULAR SCIENCE

"If a piece of physics cannot be explained to a barmaid, then it is not a good piece of physics."

ERNEST RUTHERFORD

BUT IF YOU *REALLY* WANT TO BE LISTENED TO, GET ORSON WELLES TO BROADCAST YOUR STUFF ON HALLOWEEN

The great science fiction writer H. G. Wells (1866–1946) had excellent advice for writers of "popular science":

> The reader for whom you write is just as intelligent as you are but does not possess your store of knowledge. He is not to be offended by a recital in technical language of things known to him (e.g. telling him the position of the heart and lungs and backbone). He is not a student preparing for an examination & he does not want to be encumbered with technical terms, his sense of literary form & his sense of humour are probably greater than yours.
>
> Shakespeare, Milton, Plato, Dickens, Meredith, T. H. Huxley, Darwin wrote for him. None of them are known to have talked of putting in "popular stuff" & "treating him to pretty bits" or alluded to matters as being "too complicated to discuss here." If they were, they didn't discuss them there and *that was the end of it.*

AND THAT *WAS* THE END OF IT

"Oh be quiet. Can't you see I'm busy dying?"

H. G. WELLS, ON HIS DEATHBED, TO TALKATIVE ADMIRER

JAUNDICED VIEW OF CERTAIN "SCIENCE WRITERS"

"Their idea of research is to show up with a stupid question, and ask the wrong damn person."

ANONYMOUS ARCHIVIST

FOR EXAMPLE (FROM MARK TWAIN'S *ANSWERS TO CORRESPONDENTS*)

If it would take a cannon ball $3\frac{1}{4}$ seconds to travel four miles, and $3\frac{3}{8}$ seconds to travel the next four, and $3\frac{5}{8}$ seconds to travel the next four, and if its rate of progress continued to diminish in the same ratio, how long would it take to go fifteen hundred million miles?

ARITHMETICUS
VIRGINIA, NEVADA

I don't know.

MARK TWAIN

OUR MOST POPULAR-SCIENTIFIC LIGHT BULB JOKE
How many Carl Sagans does it take to change a light bulb?
Billions and billions.

Science, Nonscience, and Antiscience

STILL NEEDED: A DEVICE TO GIVE HUMANITY POWER OVER AIRHEADS

An engineer, a physicist, a mathematician, and a mystic were asked to name the greatest invention of all time. The engineer chose fire, which gave humanity power over matter. The physicist chose the wheel, which gave humanity power over space. The mathematician chose the alphabet, which gave humanity power over symbols. The mystic chose the thermos bottle.

"Why a thermos bottle?" the others asked.

"Because the thermos keeps hot liquids hot in winter and cold liquids cold in summer."

"Yes—so what?"

"Think about it," said the mystic reverently. "That little bottle—how does it *know*?"

LIGHT BULB JOKES FOR GORILLAS . . . AND OTHER NON-
SCIENTISTS
How many gorillas does it take to change a light bulb?
Only one gorilla, but it sure takes a lot of light bulbs.

How many new-age types does it take to change a light bulb?
*Seven. Four to chant, two to give healing massages, and one to say
the bulb is really starting to look brighter*

LIGHT BULB JOKES FOR ANTISCIENTISTS
How many creationists does it take to screw in a light bulb?
Only one.
And you better believe it takes him no more than seven days.

How many pro-lifers does it take to screw in a light bulb?
Six. One to screw in the bulb,
*and five to testify that it was lit from the moment they began
screwing.*

SAM GOLDWYN'S POINT OF VIEW
"Anybody that would go to a psychiatrist ought to have his head examined."

AND SPEAKING OF BOTHERING, WHY WAS I BOTHERING *YOU*?
"Help me, doctor," the patient says to his psychiatrist. "I'm losing my memory, I can't remember anything."

"That could be serious," the doctor agrees. "How long has this been bothering you?"

"How long has what been bothering me?"

YES, BUT DON'T LAUGH IF YOU USE INDUCTIVE ARGUMENTS.
MAN: Doctor, can you help my wife? She thinks she's a chicken.
DOCTOR: Thinks she's a chicken? How long has this been going on?
MAN: For years, Doctor, for years.
DOCTOR: This is terrible! Why, you should have come to see me as soon as she started acting strangely!
MAN: Yes, but we needed the eggs!

IF HE'S AS BRILLIANT AS HE THINKS HE IS, NEXT TIME HE'LL CLAIM TO BE A HANDSOME PRINCE
Two women, out for a walk on a winter day, heard a faint croaking noise from a nearby snowbank. A frog was trapped in the snow, nearly frozen to death. One woman picked it up and warmed it gently in her hands.

Reviving, the frog began to speak. "You have saved my life! How can I ever repay you? I am, of course, no ordinary frog. Before a wicked witch transformed me, I was a brilliant scientist! Kiss me, and I shall return to my original form."

"How fascinating," said the woman, gently placing the frog in her purse and resuming her interrupted stroll.

"But aren't you going to kiss him?" asked her friend.

"Kiss him?" said the woman. "A talking frog is really worth some money!"

SCIENTISTS IN HEAVEN AND HELL

Hell

WE'D GUESS THIS GUY HAD SOME ORGANIC PROBLEM

The devil was wandering through the chemistry building late one night when he happened upon the lab of a hard-working assistant professor.

"Could I interest you in a deal?" the devil asked. "Suppose I fix things so that for the next ten years you publish every piece of research you do, ground-breaking papers every one of them. Top students clamor to work in your lab, Harvard and Yale fight to hire you, you're right at the top of the list for the Nobel Prize. But at the end of the ten years your wife will be miserable, your kids will hardly recognize your face, and you won't have a friend in the world. What would you say to that?"

The chemist thought for a moment, and then gave the devil a very skeptical look. "Okay, come out with it—what's the catch?"

BUT BOTH OF THEM FEATURE JOURNALS WITH VERY SMALL PRINT

An Egyptian scientist died and went to Hell. The devil offered him a choice. "Since you spent so much of your life at an American university, you get to choose between the Egyptian Hell and the American Hell."

"What's the difference?" asked the scientist.

"In the American Hell," the devil explained, "you get eight hours every day of being prodded with pitchforks, eight hours of being roasted on a griddle, and then eight hours of rest. In the Egyptian

Hell, you get twelve hours of pitchforks followed by twelve hours on the griddle. Which do you choose?"

But before he could choose the American Hell, the small demonic ghost of one of his former professors drifted up to his ear and whispered, "Choose the Egyptian Hell."

"Why?" asked the scientist.

"Look," hissed the ghost, "in the Egyptian Hell, sure, the demons pitchfork you a few times at the start of their shift, but then they all lie down and take a rest. And as for the griddle—we haven't had gas in a month!"

TELL HIM YOU WANT TO GO TO STEWARDESS HELL

Two scientists, call them Smith and Jones, were bitter enemies. One day, flying home from a conference where each had repeatedly denounced the other's work, they were killed in a plane crash and found themselves in Hell.

Smith awakened from blackness when a nasty-looking devil jabbed him with a pitchfork. That was bad enough. But when he spotted Jones nearby making passionate love to the beautiful stewardess, Smith let out a yell. "This is very unfair!" he cried. "Here I am being tortured and Jones is over there making love to a gorgeous blonde!"

"Shut up, you miserable sinner," said the devil, poking him again. "Who cares what *you* think of that woman's punishment?"

I WOULD FRANKLY PREFER THIS TO EGYPTIAN HELL

In his later years, Paul Erdös sometimes went hiking in the New Mexico mountains with cryptologist Gus Simmons. At one point their path skirted the top of a cliff. Erdös, preoccupied with thoughts of mathematics, hobbled along only a few feet from the precipice, until Simmons begged him to be a little careful.

Erdös smiled. "Do you know my definition of Hell?" he asked. "For a mathematician, it is falling over the edge of a cliff like this— and halfway down you *finally* figure out how to prove the Riemann hypothesis!"

A HARDY STRAIN OF PAGANISM

The number theorist G. H. Hardy (1877–1947) carried on an intense if one-sided feud with God that also came to involve the Riemann hypothesis.

Hardy was good friends with Niels Bohr, and often traveled from

England across the choppy waters of the North Sea to visit his institute. Before returning, he liked to insure his survival by sending Bohr a postcard announcing, "I have a proof for the Riemann hypothesis."

He explained his action by saying that he was confident God would never let him die with such glory!

Heaven

AND THEY WOULDN'T HAVE ROOM FOR HIS LABORATORY EITHER

A full professor from Harvard presented himself, Nobel Prize and all, at Heaven's Gate. But Saint Peter shook his head. "I'm sorry," he said, "but you'll have to go somewhere else."

"What do you mean?" demanded the professor.

Saint Peter replied sadly, "So much tenure as you expect—even we can't afford."

THE GUY WITH THE KREBS CYCLE GOT THE CHAUFFEUR TOO

Just outside the Pearly Gates, a couple of brand new angels were waiting. "Say, aren't you the Pope?" one asked the other.

"I was," said the Pope modestly. "And you?"

"A biochemist," replied his questioner.

Just then Saint Peter called their names. "Welcome to Heaven!" he said. "Your accommodations have been provided for. Your Holiness, allow me to present you the keys to a spacious suite in our Celestial Skyrise Apartments. And for you, Professor Johnson, this chauffeur is standing by to take you to your new fifty-room mansion overlooking the Garden of Eden."

Johnson climbed into his limousine and went off looking happy. The Pope turned to Saint Peter. "I don't want to seem ungrateful," he said, "but I am curious. I devoted my whole life to the service of God—why is it that I get only a suite and that other fellow receives a mansion?"

"Come on, Your Holiness," said Saint Peter. "Popes are a dime a dozen up here—how often do we get a scientist?"

AND EVEN ERDÖS WOULD AGREE

A bedraggled and chalky spirit limps up to the Pearly Gates. "What on earth have you been doing?" Saint Peter asks.

"Freshman calculus," mumbles the spirit. "I taught it for thirty-five years."

Peter swings open the gate. "Come right on in. You've been through Hell already."

SCIENTIFIC APHORISMS

"There are trivial truths and great truths. The opposite of a trivial truth is plainly false. The opposite of a great truth may be another great truth."

NIELS BOHR

"Sometimes it happens that a man's circle of horizon becomes smaller and smaller, and as the radius approaches zero it concentrates on one point. And then that becomes his point of view."

DAVID HILBERT

"It is the customary fate of new truths to begin as heresies and to end as superstitions."

T. H. HUXLEY

"Facts are the air of science. Without them you can never fly."

IVAN PAVLOV

Theorist: someone who predicts how your experiment will turn out—and then explains why it didn't.

SEIVER'S LAW OF SIMULATION

Every simulation is accompanied by an equal amount of dissimulation.

ENDORSED BY FOUR OUT OF FIVE DOCTORS, THE FIFTH IS A
BACHELOR WHO LIVES WITH MOM

When does life begin—at the moment of conception? At the moment of quickening? At the moment of birth? No, life begins when the kids are finally out of the house.

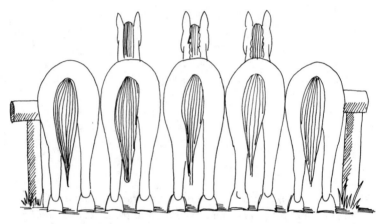

THEORY OF SPARE PARTS

There are always more horse's asses than horses.

LOSS LAW

With increasing age, memory is the second thing that goes.

"I really do not think it is any more ludicrous to believe that stones will fall through the air in some particular way or other just because Aristotle said so, than it is to believe that some kind of hair oil will make you vastly popular just because some football or baseball player says so!"

D.K.C. MACDONALD

Sex is inherited. New studies prove that if your parents never had sex, then neither will you.

LOGICAL CONCLUSIONS

A PROOF THAT THE PRINCETON EULERS ARE UNBEATABLE

(The Princeton Eulers, perhaps the world's most scientific softball team, play for the Institute for Advanced Study.)

Our proof is by induction on n, the number of games played.

First, let the number of games played be zero. Clearly, in this case our team remains undefeated.

Next, the inductive step. If we assume that the hypothesis is true when the number of games is less than n, can we show that it must follow for n games?

Suppose the team has played a season of n games. Eliminate, at random, one of these games. By our hypothesis, not one of the games in the smaller set remaining was a loss. But we have selected at random the game to be ignored. Therefore, by symmetry, not one of the n games can have resulted in defeat.

I therefore propose that we challenge the Yankees. But just to be on the safe side, in case there is a flaw in this proof, let us challenge them to a series of *only n-1* games.

LAW AND LOGIC

The Austrian logician Kurt Gödel, a refugee from the Nazis, was an unworldly man who owed much to his friends. After many years of living in this country, he was persuaded to apply for citizenship. But once Gödel began reading the American Constitution, he discovered a logical loophole that cast him into deep distress. Von Neumann had to be called in to convince him that if you looked at things the right way there would be no inconsistency.

Albert Einstein and the game theorist Oskar Morgenstern went to chaperone Gödel to the final hearing on his citizenship request. The judge was delighted to get to talk with Einstein, and they chatted at length about recent events in Nazi Germany. Finally, almost as an afterthought, the judge turned to Gödel and said, "But of course from your reading of the Constitution you now know that nothing like that could happen here."

"As a matter of fact," Gödel began—but then Morgenstern nudged him with his elbow, so Gödel got his citizenship after all.

ECONOMIC GAME THEORY, NURSERY EDITION

Bessie was one smart little kid. That's why her favorite uncle couldn't rest till he found out if the latest story about her was true. "Bessie," he said, taking two coins out of his pocket, "would you rather have this nickel or this dime?"

"Thanks, Uncle Bill, everybody knows I always take the nickel," she said, popping it into her pocket.

"That's what I heard," said her uncle, shaking his head. "Bessie, don't you know that if you take the dime you can get *two* nickels for it?"

"Sure, Uncle Bill, I know that. But don't *you* know that if I take the dime people won't keep coming up and asking me to pick?"

LOGICAL GRAFFITI

"God is dead."
   NIETZSCHE

"Nietzsche is dead."
   GOD

THE CAT WITH THREE TAILS

No cat has two tails.
But clearly, one cat has one tail more than no cat.
Therefore, at least one cat exists that has three tails.

THE IRISH FIXED-POINT THEOREM

People all over the world make fun of the Irish, but the Irish laugh at people who live in Cork County. In Cork County, people laugh at those who live in a certain town there, and those townsfolk laugh at people who live in a certain district of the town—and so on. So somewhere in Ireland there exists (God bless him!) at least one person who laughs at himself.

MATH AS A PRODUCT OF ABNORMAL SUBGROUPS

1. According to Fields Medalist Enrico Bombieri, there are three kinds of mathematicians: those who can count, and those who can't.
2. I happen to believe that people can be divided into precisely two categories—those who believe that people can be divided into precisely two categories, and those who don't.
3. If you agree with me, let me ask you this—which category is Bombieri in?

THE LOGIC OF ILLOGIC

The scene: an English tea shop.

LOGICIAN: I'd like some tea, please. Without milk.

PROPRIETOR: I'm afraid the milk has turned, Madam.

LOGICIAN: I see. Well, without lemon then.

PROOF THAT THE EARTH IS NOT FLAT

It is commonly believed that the Earth approximates a sphere and that people are walking around on the outside of that sphere.

Ridiculous!

If that were true, then the toes of people's shoes would be curved downward. Since it is well known that the toes on people's shoes are curved upward, this shows that people are actually walking around on the *inside* of the surface of a sphere.

ANTIQUE LOGICAL CIRCUIT BREAKER

"All Cretans are liars," claimed the Cretan prophet Epimenides some time around 500 B.C. Can it be true that all statements by Cretans are lies? Well, given the nationality of Epimenides, if this statement is true then it must clearly be false.

SLATKIN'S THEOREM: PROVING A CHEESE SANDWICH IS BETTER THAN ETERNAL HAPPINESS

By general agreement, nothing is better than eternal happiness.

But clearly, a cheese sandwich is better than nothing.

Therefore, a cheese sandwich is better than eternal happiness.

Science of the Impossible

IMPOSSIBILITY: THE THEOREM

From time to time, in laboratories around the world, miracles occur! Yes, that oscilloscope shows a big blip where only a small blip should be—would somebody please alert the *New York Times*? Would somebody else rewrite the laws of physics?

Some of these astounding results have turned out to be, in fact, astounding. Scientists at Bell Labs spent months scraping pigeon dung off their microwave antenna, trying to get rid of a stupid 4° Kelvin background signal. When it turned out to be a residue left not by the birds but by the Big Bang, Penzias and Wilson ended up with the Nobel Prize.

But usually the miracle turns out to be a mistake—oscilloscopes go wrong more often than physical laws. Which brings us to the simple rule of thumb developed by the physicist Sam Treiman, and known to his admirers as Treiman's Theorem: "Impossible things *usually* don't happen."

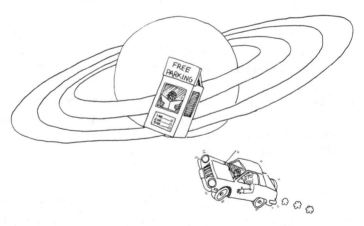

THE SCIENCE OF IF-ONLY-IT-WERE-POSSIBLE
If the universe is really expanding,
shouldn't I finally be able to find a parking space?

Afterglow

WHAT IS THIS?

Could anything be less funny than jokes that have to be explained? Yes: jokes that aren't funny even after they are explained. Of course, all the jokes in our book are funny, if you have the right turn of mind and sufficient background in science or mathematics. The purpose of this section is to supply the background—with relatively clear explanations of the humor behind some of the more obscure jokes. You'll have to supply the turn of mind.

We've intentionally left some of the jokes that presume mathematical background unexplained, as an incentive for further research. A reading that may help is listed at the end of this section.

Note to Mathematicians: Go away! Off limits! Take a vacation! DO NOT READ BEYOND THIS POINT!

MATHEMATICIAN'S NIGHTMARE LIBRARY, PAGE 37

First Aid for Dedekind Cuts. In 1872, Julius Wilhelm Richard Dedekind published a way of constructing the real numbers from the rational numbers, based on certain subsets of the rational numbers called *cuts*. Some students find the construction bloody confusing.

Jacobeans and Their Struggle for Independence. If a function f maps an open set of a Euclidean n-dimensional space into Euclidean n-dimensional space and is differentiable at a point x, the determinant of the linear operator $f'(x)$ is called the Jacobian (not the Jacobean) at x, after Carl Gustav Jacob Jacobi. If the determinant is nonzero (which some people call the case of *independence*), then f is locally invertible. All of this has nothing whatsoever to do with James I of England or the Jacobean age. Are you amused yet?

An Unabridged List of the Even Primes. This is the shortest book in the world, because it contains only the single symbol: 2. Any other even natural number is divisible by 2, so it can't be a prime.

22/7: The First 1,000 Digits. A favorite pastime of contemporary number theorists is the study of very long expansions of π, one of the most mysterious of numbers. Why mysterious? Here's an example of present ignorance about π. If π is written as $3.14\ldots$, it is not known whether the digit 1 appears infinitely often among the decimal digits in the expansion or simply stops appearing after, say, the first trillion digits. So far, billions of digits of π have been calculated, and the sequence appears to be indistinguishable from a purely random sequence of digits. On the other hand, the decimal expansion of every ratio of two whole numbers (for example, $22/7$) periodically repeats: there are no surprises or uncertainties in $22/7 = 3.142857142857\ldots$ because 142857 repeats forever. A thousand digits of such monotonies would interest only readers of sports pages, murder mysteries, and Western novels.

WHY IS 1/Z LIKE THE CATHOLIC CHURCH?, PAGE 38.

In case you haven't noticed, the current Pope is a Pole, and one of beatific simplicity. On the other hand, when z approaches 0 (the center of the plane of complex numbers), $1/z$ increases toward infinity (Heavenward, as it were), and the technical term for this singular behavior is a "simple pole."

LET Y = NUMBER OF X IT TAKES TO CHANGE A LIGHT BULB, PAGE 40

Constructive mathematicians. Constructive mathematicians do not work on construction sites. Constructive mathematics is based on the finitary standpoint, a concept introduced by David Hilbert (of whom more below) in an effort to show that mathematics is free of internal contradictions. The finitary standpoint accepts as legitimate only facts expressible in a finite number of symbols and only procedures that can be completed in a finite number of steps. The finitary standpoint excludes the limiting procedures typical of calculus as well as the approximation of any continuous object or action in terms of infinitely many infinitesimal elements. One might say that constructive mathematicians would only change a light bulb if it could be turned by jerks.

Number theorists. Around 1637 (mighty Harvard was one year old then), Pierre de Fermat was reading a Latin translation of Diophantus' *Arithmetika*. Diophantus discusses the problem of finding all trios x, y, and z of whole numbers that satisfy the Pythagorean formula $x^2 + y^2 = z^2$ for right triangles. (Surely you remember the Pythagorean formula from high school? If not, do you remember high school?) In the margin next to the Pythagorean formula, Fermat wrote that if n is any whole number larger than 2, then there are no whole numbers x, y, and z, all different from 0, such that $x^n + y^n = z^n$. He then added what has become the most famous marginal notation in all of mathematics, and perhaps in all of science: "I have discovered a truly remarkable proof of this theorem which this margin is too small to contain." No one knows whether Fermat really had a proof of what is generally known as "Fermat's last theorem," but it is certain that no one since Fermat has been able to find a proof, despite centuries of strenuous efforts. Since a theorem is a mathematical statement that has been proved, Fermat's last theorem may or may not be a theorem. Mathematicians take small comfort in knowing that Fermat's assertion is true at least for $n \leq 30{,}000$.

Classical geometers. Classical geometry allows only constructions that use no tools other than a straightedge and a compass. One famous problem that cannot be solved with these tools is to find a square with the same area as a given circle. (Here, π rears another of its Medusa heads.)

Have you noticed the resemblance between classical geometry and the finitary standpoint of Hilbert? Both are like trying to build a space shuttle with a screwdriver, or writing a novel with a dull pencil held between your teeth while your arms are tied behind your back and you stand on rollerskates. Mathematicians love to see what they can accomplish with a limited set of tools under restrictive conditions. The results are often astounding.

WORLD'S MOST SELF-REFERENTIAL LIGHT BULB JOKES, PAGE 40

Gödel number. In 1931, Kurt Gödel proved a famous incompleteness theorem about mathematics and logic by constructing a formula A which may be viewed as asserting that A is unprovable, and showing that neither A nor the contradictory of A is provable in the formal language in which A is expressed. Clear enough? Gödel's proof uses a procedure for translating each statement in the formal language into a positive whole number. That number is now called the Gödel number of the statement. My theory is that if a light bulb is bright enough to know its own Gödel number then it doesn't need to be changed.

MATHEMATICAL TOMBSTONE TERRITORY, PAGE 42

David Hilbert. At an international congress of mathematicians held in Paris in 1900, Hilbert stated 23 problems as targets for twentieth-century mathematics. To solve one of Hilbert's problems is to be guaranteed mathematical immortality. One of his problems was solved the same year he proposed it; others still remain sources of cheerful torment to the mathematical tribe. Among the latter, problem 8 is one of the most famous; it is to show the correctness of the Riemann hypothesis. This problem is so important to mathematics that it receives *two* jokes all of its own in this book (see below).

Werner Heisenberg. His uncertainty principle says that the more precisely you determine the position of a particle, the less precisely you can determine its momentum or velocity; the more precisely you determine the velocity of a particle, the less precisely you can determine its exact position. So if we know precisely where Werner lies, we can't be sure where Werner is going (unless, of course, he lies).

Henri Léon Lebesgue. He developed approaches to measuring volume (in spaces more abstract than ordinary Euclidean space) which are now called the Lebesgue integral or Lebesgue measure. Presumably his favorite Shakespeare play was *Measure for Measure.*

Godefrey Herold Hardy. Among the best-known books written by this number theorist, analyst, and elegant writer is *A Mathematician's Apology.*

Stefan Banach. He developed the theory of the abstract spaces that now bear his name.

Georg Cantor. Cantor created the concept of cardinal numbers and proved that there are more transcendental than algebraic numbers. He introduced the use of aleph, the first letter of the Hebrew alphabet, to indicate the cardinality of a transfinite initial ordinal number. When his theory came under attack from the mathematician Kronecker, Cantor wrote: "The essence of mathematics lies in its freedom!" He practiced what he preached.

Pierre de Fermat. Already you're an expert on Fermat, right?

A COMPOSITE OF PROOFS THAT ALL ODD NUMBERS ARE PRIME, PAGE 53

Let me break this to you gently. 9 is an odd number that is not prime. A prime number is a natural number (e.g., 1, 2, 3, . . .) that cannot be written as the product of two natural numbers (not necessarily different) both of which are bigger than 1. In this case, $9 = 3 \times 3$. A number that is not prime is called composite. Even this joke's title is a joke.

DEGREES CABLE?, PAGE 76

The centigrade scale divides the difference between the freezing point and the boiling point of water into 100 equal steps or degrees, and assigns 0° C to freezing and 100°C to boiling. Degrees Celsius (after Anders Celsius) are the same as degrees centigrade. The Kelvin scale measures temperature differences using centigrade (or Celsius) degrees, but assigns the freezing point of water to 273.16°K and absolute zero temperature to 0°K. Imagine the confusion if William Thomson (Lord Kelvin) had chosen a title like Lord Cable or Lord Compass, or even Lord Cohen. (Probably the risk of adopting the last of these three names was small.)

MORE MATHEMATICIANS CLAIM TO DO IT—AND HOW!, PAGE 109

Differential Topologists typically deal with differentiable functions; that is, functions that are *smooth* enough to have derivatives.

Algebraic Topologists study manifolds. Loosely speaking, an n-dimensional topological manifold is a space that looks locally like (is homeomorphic to) an n-dimensional Euclidean space or an n-dimensional Euclidean half-space. For example, the ordinary plane of plane geometry is a 2-dimensional manifold.

Group Theorists have devoted immense efforts in recent decades to classifying the so-called simple groups. A simple group is one with no normal subgroup other the group itself and the identity element. Is that simple enough for you?

Software Engineers use I/O for "input/output." Any connection with anatomy is all in your mind.

In 1907, Andrei Andreevic Markov (1856–1922, not to be confused with the mathematician of the same name born in 1903) introduced an immensely useful probabilistic model now called a *Markov chain*. A Markov chain describes a sequence of events in which the past and the future are conditionally independent, given the present. If the weather were a Markov chain, and if you knew today's weather, you would learn nothing more about the probability distribution of tomorrow's weather by additional knowledge of the weather in the past. Markov chains have been used to model sequences of letters in written texts, sequences of bases in DNA, learning, states of health and illness, the weather, stream flows, animal behavior, and lots more.

Pierre de Fermat. See above.

The first volume of *Norbert Wiener*'s autobiography is called *Ex-Prodigy.* Read it.

Carl Friedrich Gauss was a mathematical genius of the late eighteenth and early nineteenth century who is held in awe by today's mathematicians. André Weil's history of number theory stops before Gauss. When asked why he didn't continue and write a second volume, Weil reportedly answered, "Then I would have to write about Gauss."

BUT HIS ARGUMENT WAS THE RIGHT ONE, PAGE 131

The stability of linear dynamical systems is determined by the location in the complex plane of the roots or poles of a characteristic equation. When all the poles are in the left half-plane, the real parts are all negative and oscillations damp out with increasing time, so the stability of the system is assured.

Nevertheless, for your comfort and safety, you are advised to keep your seat-belt fastened about you and remain seated until the plane has come to a complete stop, preferably after moving in a horizontal and not vertical direction.

I WOULD FRANKLY PREFER THIS TO EGYPTIAN HELL, PAGE 146

and

A HARDY STRAIN OF PAGANISM, PAGE 146

Just what is the Riemann hypothesis, goad of so many mathematicians even to this day? Roll up your sleeves, spit on your hands, and get ready for some work. Georg Friedrich Bernhard Riemann's ζ-function (ζ is pronounced "zeta") is given by (eek! eek! a real formula! eek!)

$$\zeta(z) = 1 + \frac{1}{2^z} + \frac{1}{3^z} + \ldots \frac{1}{n^z} + \ldots$$

where z is any real or complex number. A zero of Riemann's ζ-function is any number z such that $\zeta(z) = 0$. Riemann's ζ-function has infinitely many zeros for which the real part exceeds 0 and is less than 1. Riemann conjectured in 1859 that every single one of these zeros has a real part exactly equal to ½. (From this he makes a living?)

Our old friend Hardy proved in 1914 that infinitely many zeros of Riemann's ζ-function have a real part exactly equal to ½. The first several million zeros all have a real part exactly equal to ½; the count increases every so often. If you find a proof of Riemann's conjecture, call me collect. Immediately.

Admit it, guys and gals: this is a joke book with class! Did you ever think you'd see a joke book with the formula for Riemann's ζ-function in it? Use this joke book to impress your friends and persuade your mother that you're improving your mind!

A PROOF THAT THE PRINCETON EULERS ARE UNBEATABLE, PAGE 151

Leonhard Euler's last name is pronounced "oiler." I think it's also the name of a professional athletic team, but I'm not sure. Athletic teams are beyond the scope of this book.

FOR FURTHER AMUSEMENT

If you have read this far, you are wasting your time reading joke books; you should be reading mathematics and science books. Put this away immediately and get to work! If you want to roam among the high peaks of mathematics, I recommend highly (!) the *Encyclopedic Dictionary of Mathematics* (MIT Press, Cambridge, Massachusetts, second edition, 1987, 4 volumes), prepared by the Mathematical Society of Japan. Even the two-volume first edition (1977) is a marvel. Everything is there, but it's lean cuisine. When used in combination with this joke book, the *Encyclopedic Dictionary of Mathematics* offers a fantastic mathematical education.

—J.E.C.

Dirac anecdotes (pp. 59, 68). From *Reminiscences About a Great Physicist: Paul Adrien Maurice Dirac*, Behram N. Kursonoglu and Eugene T. Wigner, editors, Cambridge University Press, 1987. Reprinted by permission of Cambridge University Press.

Von Neumann quotes and anecdotes (p. 84). Reprinted from "The Legacy of John von Neumann," by Peter D. Lax, *Proceedings of Symposia of Pure Mathematics*, Volume 50, 1990, by permission of the American Mathematical Society.

Mathematicians ". . . do it . . ." (p. 109). Reprinted from "How Mathematicians Do It," by Robert J. Lipshutz, *Mathematical Intelligencer*, 13(3):55, (1991) by permission of Springer-Verlag and Robert J. Lipshutz.

Agassiz anecdotes (pp. 13, 36). From *Louis Agassiz: A Life in Science*, by Edward Lurie. The Johns Hopkins University Press, Baltimore/London, 1980. Copyright © 1988 Edward Lurie. Reprinted by permission of The Johns Hopkins University Press.

Lord Kelvin anecdotes (p. 76), MacDonald quote (p. 150). From *Faraday, Maxwell, and Kelvin*, by D. K. C. MacDonald, Doubleday & Company (Anchor Books), 1964. Reprinted by permission of Doubleday, a division of Bantam, Doubleday, Dell Publishing Group, Inc.

Lavoisier anecdote (p. 138). From *Antoine Lavoisier and the Revolution in Chemistry*, Rebecca B. Markus, Franklin Watts & Co., 1964.

Lefschetz translation (p. 77). Reprinted from "Solomon Lefschetz: An Appreciation in Memoriam," by Lawrence Markus, *Bulletin of the American Mathematical Society*, Volume 79, 1973, by permission of the American Mathematical Society.

Curie anecdotes (pp. 135–6). From *Marie Curie*, by Robin McKown. Copyright © 1959 by Robin McKown.

Einstein couplet (p. 81), Einstein anecdote (p. 101), Harvey anecdote (p. 110), Humboldt anecdote (pp. 73–4), Voltaire quote (p. 80). From *The Great Scientists*, Jack Meadows, Oxford University Press, 1987.

Lord Kelvin (p. 77), Alexander the Great (p. 95), Euclid (p. 105), Bolyai (p. 139) anecdotes. From *On Mathematics and Mathematicians*, Robert Edouard Moritz, Dover Publications, Inc. Reprinted by permission of Dover Publications, Inc.

Alexander (p. 16), Erdös (p. 17), and Lefschetz (p. 77) anecdotes. From *The Princeton Mathematics Community in the 1930s: An Oral History Project*. Frederick Nebeker, Editor. Copyright © 1985 by the Trustees of Princeton University. Administrator, Charles C. Gillispie, interviewers, Albert W. Tucker and William Aspray. Excerpts printed with permission of Professor Charles Gillispie, Professor A. W. Tucker, Ben Reimer, Archivists, and Jean Mahoney, Manager of Technical Transfer.

Computer expert jokes (p. 28), Millikan's housekeeper (p. 103), and Morse (p. 103) anecdotes. From *Funny Business: Speaker's Treasury of Business Humor for All Occasions*, by Gene Perret and Linda Perret. Copyright © 1990. Used by permission of the publisher, Prentice-Hall/A Division of Simon & Schuster, Englewood Cliffs, NJ.

Infinite loop, big microcomputer (p. 27), economist knows, trouble (p. 30) glacier (pp. 33–4), marriage (p. 63), lunch (p. 140), light bulb with health insurance (p. 115), little patients (p. 118) jokes. Taken from *The All-New Clean Joke Book*, by Bob Phillips. Copyright © 1990 by Harvest House Publishers, Eugene, Oregon, 97042. Used by permission.

Courant anecdotes (p. 106). From *Courant in Göttingen and New York*, Constance Reid, Springer-Verlag, 1976. Reprinted by permission of Springer-Verlag.

Hilbert anecdotes (pp. 73, 135, 149) and Hardy anecdote (pp. 146–47). From *Hilbert*, Constance Reid, Springer-Verlag, 1970. Reprinted by permission of Springer-Verlag.

Bohr anecdotes (pp. 19, 64, 89). From *Niels Bohr: His Life and Work as Seen by His Friends and Colleagues*, S. Rozental, editor, John Wiley & Sons, 1967. By permission of Elsevier Science Publishers BV.

Einstein hair anecdote (pp. 72–3). From *Einstein in America*, by Jamie Sayen, Crown Publishing, 1985. Permission granted by the Albert Einstein Archives, the Hebrew University of Jerusalem, Israel.